Taking Sides

and Related Readings

McDougal Littell
A HOUGHTON MIFFLIN COMPANY
Evanston, Illinois • Boston • Dallas

Acknowledgments

Harcourt Brace & Company: *Taking Sides* by Gary Soto. Copyright © 1991 by Gary Soto. Reprinted by permission of Harcourt Brace & Company.

Terry D. Allen: "Endless Search" by Alonzo Lopez, from *The Whispering Wind: Poetry by Young American Indians*, edited by Terry D. Allen. Used by permission of the author.

University of Notre Dame Press: Excerpt from *Barrio Boy* by Ernesto Galarza. Copyright © 1971 by the University of Notre Dame Press. Reprinted by permission of the publisher.

BOA Editions, Ltd.: "in the inner city," from *Good Woman: Poems and a Memoir 1969–1980* by Lucille Clifton. Copyright © 1987 by Lucille Clifton. Reprinted with the permission of BOA Editions, Ltd., Rochester, NY.

María Teresa S. Sánchez: "i yearn" by Ricardo Sánchez. Reprinted by permission of María Teresa S. Sánchez.

Children's Better Health Institute: "Granny Ed and the Lewisville Raiders" by Rae Rainey, from *Young World*, 1977. Copyright © 1977 by Review Publishing Company. Used by permission of Children's Better Health Institute, Benjamin Franklin Literary & Medical Society, Inc., Indianapolis, Indiana.

Cover illustration by Keith Skeen.
Background photograph (basketball) Copyright © PhotoDisc.

Printed in the United States of America.

ISBN 0-395-88140-4

11 12 13 14 15 16 17 18 – DCI – 09 08 07 06 05 04

Contents

Taking Sides

Gary Soto

For Jim, Jr. and Marty, two players

Chapter 1

"Tony," Lincoln Mendoza whispered into the telephone. "It's your buddy, Linc."

"Linc? My homeboy moved to the good side of town," Tony Contreras answered sleepily.

It was 7:15 Thursday morning. The rising sun hurled a spear of light through Lincoln's kitchen window. His dog, Flaco, lay still, bathing in the warm rays, his ribs slowly rising and falling. His mother was in the shower, singing along with the radio.

"Be serious, *ese*. We're playin' you next Tuesday," Lincoln said, moving the receiver from one hand to the other.

There was a pause and the squeak of bedsprings. Tony was sitting up. "Do you know what time it is? It's early, *hombre*. It's still dark."

"Not if you open your eyes. It's time to crack those books," Lincoln said.

"Books? Yeah, I'm gonna crack 'em over my little brother's head, the *menso*. He spilled a soda on my bed."

"Leave him alone. He's just a punk," Lincoln said then changed the subject back to basketball. "It's gonna be weird playin' Franklin for real."

Lincoln was a star basketball player, tall but not thin. When he made a fist, his forearm tightened with muscles. His stomach was muscle, his legs muscle. His face was brown, like coffee laced with cream, and his hair black as a chunk of asphalt. People said he was handsome, but Lincoln wasn't really sure.

He had moved from the Mission District of San Francisco, an urban barrio, to Sycamore, a pleasant suburban town with tree-lined streets. His mother had gotten tired of yanking open her drapes to see run-down Chevys and fender-buckled Ford Torinos bleeding black oil. Tired of the ghetto blasters shouldered by shirtless *vatos*. Tired of jackhammers cutting up the street early in the morning. Tired of the Number 43 bus leaving shreds of black smoke hovering in the dank city air. It was time to get out, she said one day when she came home from work and found her planter box tipped over, her snapdragons stomped, and her small Victorian flat ransacked. The window screen was slashed, and the TV and stereo were gone. Left in their place were a couple of crushed beer cans and cigarette butts.

So they had moved to a small two-bedroom house with a yard and a mulberry tree whose fruit left purple splotches on the sidewalk. Lincoln was now an eighth grader. The move was a voyage of ten miles south from San Francisco to a place where the better homes stood in the sunlight of wealth and sent Lincoln from Franklin Junior High to Columbus Junior High.

"How are the *vatos* at school?" Lincoln asked.

"OK."

"Are they mad at me?"

"*¿Por qué?*"

"You know, movin' away. Like my new school playin' you *vatos*?"

Tony groaned. "You kiddin'? No one's mad. If we had money, we'd get out too."

"That's what you think. This place is dead. No one ever comes out of the house to check out the world."

"Yeah, but that's the problem here. No one stays

home. There's cop sirens every night." Then Tony asked, "How's Flaco? Mom said he got hit."

"Flaco's workin' on three legs. He's OK." Lincoln turned to Flaco, snapped his fingers, and asked, "You're cool, huh, Flaco?"

Flaco raised his head and looked at Lincoln. His left leg was a balloon of bandages from a hit-and-run motorcycle accident. He lowered his head slowly and went back to sleep.

Lincoln and Tony talked about school, friends, fights behind backstops, Lincoln's ex-girlfriend Vicky, and basketball, which they now played for different schools.

Lincoln heard the shower stop and the curtain pull back.

"I wish I could be smashin' the boards for your school. Your uniforms are sweet-lookin'," Tony said. "Anyway, you guys are in first and we're next to last."

"For me, it's the other way around," Lincoln said. "I'd rather be playin' for Franklin, not Columbus. There's no brown people here. Everyone's white, except for one black dude on the team. And our coach is a nasty dude. He's got trouble inside his head."

In the bedroom, a hair dryer began whirring.

"Maybe you can come over Saturday?" Tony asked. "Play some hoop or something?"

"I guess. But I gotta go now. Check you later."

Lincoln hung up and poured a small pile of dog food onto the floor, prompting Flaco to drag himself to his crunchies. Then he got himself a glass of milk and fixed some toast, which he chewed thoughtfully while looking at pictures of Egypt in his geography book.

He admired the Sphinx, basking forever under the hot sun, and marveled at the Nile, a dark river that seemed to oppose gravity by flowing north. He looked closely at a camel driver smiling into the camera. The camel driver's teeth were rotten and his face was lined from working in the sun.

He closed the book when his mother came into the kitchen, her face flushed from a hot shower. She was rubbing lotion into the backs of her hands.

"*Mi'jo*, you have to eat more than toast," she said, tying her robe tighter. "*¿Quieres un huevo?* You want an egg?"

"I'm not hungry," he said. "We're playing Franklin next Tuesday. Can you come?"

"I'll see." She made herself a cup of coffee, joined Lincoln at the table, and opened her glossy appointment book.

"I may be home late that day," she said, scribbling a note to herself. "*No sé, mi'jo.*"

"You're working hard, huh, Mom?"

"Yeah, I'm working like crazy."

His mother was a graphic artist who for ten years had worked for an advertising firm in San Francisco. She was now her own boss. She had started a business, at first named after herself, Beatrice Mendoza Graphics. Later she settled on calling it On-the-Line Graphics, a fancier name. Her business accounts were strong from the start, and getting better, with six clients in computer-rich Silicon Valley.

"Come on, Mom," he begged. "Just this once. It's Franklin we're playin'."

"Wipe your mouth. It has milk around it," she said. She closed her book, sipped from her Have-a-Nice-Day coffee cup, and said she would try but couldn't promise.

Lincoln wiped his mouth with the back of his hand. He got up from his chair and called Flaco, who rose slowly, wagging his tail. They went outside to the front yard. The sun leaked through the neighbor's eucalyptus tree, whose top swayed from a wind that seldom touched ground. A leaf fluttered to the lawn, and Lincoln picked it up and sniffed it. He liked the smell and crushed the leaf in his palm.

He watched the neighbors, most of them dressed in suits, start off to their jobs in BMWs, Saabs, and Volvos with their private-school sons and daughters in the backseats. Lincoln and a basketball friend were the only kids on the block who went to Columbus Junior High, the public school. He thought of waving to one of the cars as it passed, but he only looked and kicked the dry gravel at his feet.

When he had arrived in the new neighborhood, Lincoln had liked the peacefulness of sprinklers hissing on green lawns and the sycamores that lined the street. He liked the splashes of flowers and neatly piled firewood. He liked the hedges where jays built scrawny nests and bickered when cats slithered too close. The people seemed distant, but that was fine with him. It was better than the loud cars that raced up and down his old block. It was better than littered streets and graffiti-covered walls that called out "*Con safos*" and "F-14."

Now, three months later, Lincoln was having second thoughts. He missed his old school and its mural of brown, black, and yellow kids linking arms in friendship. He had liked Franklin Junior High, tough as it was, with its fights in the hallways and in the noisy cafeteria. He had liked to walk among brown faces and stand with the Vietnamese and Korean kids. He missed his friends, especially his number-one man, Tony Contreras, whom he had known forever, even before first grade when Tony accidentally knocked out Lincoln's front baby teeth going down the slide. And he missed Vicky. They had parted on bad terms, but Lincoln felt that if he could speak with her everything would turn out OK.

Three weeks ago he had played against his old school in a nonleague basketball game, and he had scored twelve points and made five rebounds and three assists. Columbus had whipped Franklin, and he felt bad for his old school. He felt bad at how most of the guys from Franklin wore K-mart sneakers while Columbus team members squeaked about the court in Air Jordans. It's not fair, he thought, but what can I do?

Lincoln looked down at his watch: 7:45. He was about to go back inside when he saw James, his basketball friend, a second-stringer at Columbus.

James hurried across the street, two doughnuts in his hand. "Lincoln, where are your shoes?"

Lincoln looked down at his rubber thongs. His big toe was purple from the time he dunked a ball and came down hard.

"Hey, James," Lincoln said.

James raised his doughnut as if to ask "Want some?" Lincoln thought of basketball practice as he tore off a piece of doughnut and chewed it slowly, the sweet grit of sugar between his teeth.

"What's your dog's name again?" James asked. "Rocko?"

"No, dude, Flaco."

They were silent for a moment as they watched their breath hang in the winter air. James asked, "What does 'Flaco' mean?"

"Skinny."

James gave the rest of the doughnut to Flaco and said, "He doesn't look skinny to me."

"That's 'cause he likes doughnuts."

James licked his fingers, wiped them on his pants, and said, "We play your old school again, don't we?"

"Yeah," Lincoln said. He wished James hadn't brought it up. He pictured his friends from Franklin wildly stomping their feet in the bleachers and screaming "*vendido*" at him, the former homeboy. He pictured Coach Ramos throwing himself into a folding chair, his hands covering his tired face. He felt like a traitor.

They stood in silence looking at Flaco rolling his tongue over his mouth. Grains of sugar spotted his black nose.

When he heard his mom calling, Lincoln said he had to go. He and Flaco raced up the steps and James walked away, leaving shoeprints on the wet lawn.

"I'm late already," his mother said, brushing her hair roughly in front of the hallway mirror. "I've got to get to San Jose by nine."

Lincoln poured himself another glass of milk, drank quickly with an eye on the clock, and for a split second watched a hummingbird at the kitchen window pause and dart from the feeder without drinking.

"I'm going to be at basketball practice," Lincoln said.

His mother, searching frantically for her keys in her purse, didn't look up as she said, "Have fun."

Fun, Lincoln thought. That's a new way of putting it.

While Flaco lounged in the puddle of sunlight that had moved from the kitchen floor to the living room, Lincoln put on his shoes, brushed his teeth, and combed his hair in front of the full-length mirror on his closet door. He waved to his mom, who was juggling two briefcases and a plastic tube of drawings. She smiled at him and said, "Bye, *mi'jo*. Don't forget to peel some *papas* when you get home."

Chapter 2

Columbus Junior High was a stucco group of pink and green buildings and a track the color of rust. The grass, like the grass at other schools, was mostly brown. The trash cans were buckled, but no candy wrappers or potato-chip bags scuttled across the campus. Cedar trees stood in front of the administration building, and a thorny pyracantha separated the boys' and girls' locker rooms. A statue of Christopher Columbus with a telescope to his eye stood in front of the school, where the principal, Mr. Kimball, often waited at first bell with fistfuls of tardy slips. On a good day, he managed to hand out only two. The kids were well behaved, and the daily worries among the teachers were tardiness, lost jackets, and occasional fights in the hallway.

The kids dressed stylishly. When they smiled, their teeth gleamed with braces. It would never enter their minds to shop at K-mart or tote a bologna sandwich in a twice-used paper bag. Lincoln opted to live a simple life. His bologna sandwich, along with an apple and some chips, sat in his backpack, crushed between his geography and math books.

His mother harangued him about his clothes, but he wore jeans, busted at the knees, and his coat was a hand-me-down from an uncle. The front of Lincoln's shirt was splotched blue where he once let his Bic pen ride in the pocket during a wash.

Lincoln sighed and entered the school grounds. Just two more days to the weekend.

Mr. Green, the algebra teacher, scribbled x's and y's on the chalkboard. Lincoln copied the math problems and followed along, figuring out the first two, the easiest. But he bit his pencil in frustration because the rest were impossible.

"If you figure y is equal to $2x$, then you can see that x is obviously smaller than the value of y," Mr. Green rambled.

That's easy for you to say, Lincoln thought. You got the book with the answers to work from.

"And if you recall, we worked out $2x$ plus $2xy$ minus $3y$," Mr. Green droned on.

Lincoln's stomach tightened around his hunger. I should have had more than toast, he thought. He pushed the heel of his palm into his stomach until the growling stopped. But when it started again, the girl sitting next to him smirked. He smiled and said, "I missed breakfast."

After algebra, there were history and Spanish. At lunch he ate alone, scribbling out his homework for English, which was mostly recognizing the parts of speech. He thought it was funny how the teacher, Mrs. Baker, said the same things over and over. "A chair is a noun; a beach umbrella is a noun. Is Bobby a noun?"

Bobby was the dumbest kid in the class. He couldn't figure out if he was a verb or a noun, and whenever the teacher called on him he said, "I dunno," before the question was finished. No one liked Bobby.

Lincoln bit into his sandwich roughly. He opened his geography book and once again the guy on the camel was smiling his lined face at him. He's like me, Lincoln thought. Brown as earth and no one knows his name. He closed the book when a basketball play came to his mind.

"Cut right, left, and a dribble pass to the forward," he muttered to himself. He took another bite of his bologna sandwich and looked up to see James with a girl. Lincoln wiped his mouth, cleared his throat, and said to James, "Hey, homes." To the girl, he said, "Hi."

The girl was nearly as tall as James. She had short dark hair, almost like a boy's. But she was no boy. She was good to look at, and that's what Lincoln did as the two of them pulled up chairs. James said, "This is Monica Torres. Monica, this is Lincoln, ah, let me see. What's your last name, Linc?"

"Mendoza."

"That's right, Linc Mendoza, star basketball player."

Monica smiled as she sat down. "James said you went to Franklin. I used to go there."

"Really?" Lincoln asked, curious, his eyebrows raised. "I don't remember you."

"Well, I did, for two months," she said. "But we moved here. My dad didn't like me going to school in the city."

"But your dad didn't have to go to school."

"It's true. But you know how Franklin is."

"You mean nasty."

"That's one way of putting it."

"That's the only way of putting it."

Lincoln wanted to tell her about the Franklin he knew, but how could he keep the conversation polite? He didn't want to tell her that he had had to visit knuckle city himself a couple of times, or about the times he'd walked home holding a bloody nose, or the loose tooth with its string of blood, or the pink scar on his chin from an uppercut.

He pushed aside his lunch bag. He wiped his mouth with his napkin, just to be sure, and looked at

James. "We beat Franklin pretty bad last time, didn't we?"

"Does a polar bear live in snow? By a mile, and I scored nine points."

"Yeah," Lincoln said, and then, looking at Monica, he jerked his thumb at James and asked, "Is James in one of your classes?"

"*En* Spanish. *Tengo que ayudarle. Es medio tonto.*"

"*De veras. Pero cuando juega el basketbol, James—*"

James said, "Hey, what's the jive? Speak English, Linc, or I won't help you stay a star."

"*Oye a este chavalo.* Listen to this guy. I'm helping *him* stay second-string."

James almost laughed and said, "Yeah, it's true. Linc's pretty good. You should see his outside shot."

Monica's face brightened. "I used to play for the girls' team."

"Really?" Lincoln asked, surprised.

"Yeah, *really.*" She smiled and folded her sweater on her lap. "I played forward at Franklin for a while, but Coach Nagel—remember her?—switched me to guard."

"Coach Nagel. I almost forgot about her." Lincoln leaned back into his chair. He pictured Coach Nagel lifting weights with the boys after school. She was pretty cool. "Wow, you played hoop. For Franklin, too."

"Yeah, I played hoop. You don't seem to believe me."

"Oh, yeah, I believe you. It's just that I've never met anyone from here who went to Franklin—and played basketball."

Monica looked down at the table and brushed

away a few of Lincoln's sandwich crumbs. "That was last year. But I had to quit. Mom said I was too busy."

Lincoln crushed his lunch bag into a ball and tossed it at James, who batted it away.

"I take piano," Monica continued, "and my dad makes me take aikido."

"What's aikido?"

"A martial art. It's pretty boring."

"Too bad. So you gave up basketball?"

Monica clicked her polished nails against the tabletop and said, "More or less. But sometimes I play at the elementary school near my house."

Lincoln and James looked at each other. "Where?" they asked in unison.

Monica got to her feet, cuddling her books and sweater, without answering. "I have homework to do. Our teacher makes us write a page a day in a diary. Sometimes I don't know what to write so I just put down what I ate or what I saw on television. I had spaghetti for lunch today. I wonder how I can write something interesting about that."

"Maybe you can say that the spaghetti looked purple," James said. "Mine did, at least. Maybe it's the onions."

Monica smiled, and her face crinkled up. "Purple? You're strange, James."

Lincoln and James stood as she started to leave.

"I hope you can come to the game next Tuesday," Lincoln asked. "We're playin' Franklin."

"That'd be super. I'll try," Monica said as she peeled back her cuff to look at her watch. Lincoln noticed that she wore a heart-shaped ring on her left hand. A boyfriend, he thought. Or something she picked up on her own? Maybe her mom bought it for her?

"I have fifteen minutes to write three pages," she said. "*Mucho gusto en conocerte.* Nice to meet you, Lincoln."

She walked away, leaving Lincoln and James staring at her. They looked at each other and both said at once, "She's cute. And she plays basketball."

"Did you really get to know her in Spanish?" Lincoln asked, crushing his milk carton with a blow of his fist. Milk sprayed onto the table.

"She saved me from a couple of D's, or worse. She knows her stuff. She must be full Mexican."

Lincoln made a face at James, who was hurling the crushed milk carton into a trash can. "What do you mean, 'full Mexican'? You sound dumb."

Lincoln rose to his feet, the chair scraping loudly against the floor, and said good-bye by punching James in the arm—hard. He had no place to go except out into the hallway, where he spent the remainder of the lunch period softly banging every third locker with his fist and thinking of Monica doing jump shots from twenty feet out.

Chapter 3

"Drive! Step on it! Move an elbow into his face!" Coach Yesutis yelled from the edge of the court. Moisture darkened his underarms and gathered on his brow. Sweat made his thinning hair flatten and hang down.

For the coach, watching his players was as exhausting as playing. He ran up and down the court, shouting plays through cupped hands and slapping a clipboard against his thighs when a play was executed poorly. The two-hour workouts were intense. Shafts of afternoon sunlight glared on the polished gym floor. Today's practice featured the A-team, the first-stringers, against the B-team, the players who sat on the bench chewing their fingernails during the regular games.

"Come on, Durkins, get in his face," the coach scolded. "Mendoza, move your can."

The basketball echoed in the Columbus Junior High School gym, where banners of the team's championship years—1980, 1987, and 1989—hung from the rafters.

"Bukowski, breathe on him. Maneuver left—now cut, Grady! Press!"

Shoes squeaked as the players hustled up and down the court. The fluorescent lights hummed overhead, and the heater blew warm, dusty air. A few students sat cross-legged on the floor, books piled in their laps, watching. In a far corner, three cheerleaders bounced from foot to foot, chanting

"Hey! Hey! Whatta you say!" It was practice hour for them, too.

Lincoln blew past the center, Grady, and, leaping to his left, slammed the ball through the hoop. He came down hard, jamming his already-hurt toe. He stopped for a moment, grimacing, then hobbled after the other players, a spark of pain flashing in his foot.

"Come on!" Coach hissed, as he ran his hands through his hair.

He blew a whistle that hung on a chain around his wrist and whacked his clipboard against his thigh. The players came to a stop. The sound of their breathing filled the gym as they stood with hands on their hips. One player knelt down on one knee, but he rose when Coach gave him an angry look. The cheerleaders, oblivious to the game, raised their arms and screamed.

"Mendoza, take a seat. Buckley, come in."

Lincoln trotted slowly to the bench, where he took a seat between the two remaining players, both second-stringers with skinny legs, and smothered his face in a towel. A thin line of sweat snaked down his arm. The hair on his thighs was matted to his skin. He took off his left shoe and sock and rubbed his toe gingerly. He turned to the player who was keeping score and asked, "How many buckets did I get?"

The player looked down at his score sheet. "Four. And two free throws. How's your leg?"

"It's my toe. Hurts bad."

The two of them looked briefly at the toe and then turned their attention back to the game. The A-team was up by seven, 22–15. Coach is gonna be upset, Lincoln thought. The A-team should be clobbering the second-stringers.

Lincoln wiped his face and froze when the coach said, "Mendoza, put your shoe back on! Who do you think you are? Someone special? Magic Johnson? James Worthy?"

"I hurt my toe. . . ."

"Poor boy, he hurt his itsy-bitsy toe."

None of the players laughed with the coach.

Lincoln stared angrily at the coach, who turned away with a smirk. Who do you think *you* are? Lincoln thought as he slipped his hurt foot back into his shoe. A spark of pain flared when he tugged on the laces.

Lincoln couldn't understand why Coach was always on his back. He was always on time to practice, and he was never a loudmouth like Bukowski or Durkins. He never complained about his injuries, either. In last week's game, the one that kept Columbus in the league race, he got jabbed in the eye—on purpose, he thought, because he was slamming at the boards. But he just blinked until the pain lessened, and he let his eye tear until his vision returned to normal. Another time he sprained a finger, but that didn't stop him from scoring thirteen points.

Lincoln grunted as he yanked at his laces, sweat dripping from his face and dotting the floor around him. He breathed in deeply and jogged slowly back to center court along with two guys from the bench. Immediately, Lincoln scored a basket on a sweet, three-second-in-the-air lay-up, but he was fouled with a stinging slap to the wrist. He missed at the free-throw line, and for the remaining minutes of the first half he went without another basket.

At halftime, the coach went into his office to use the telephone. He returned a few minutes later to scold the players for their poor defense and slow breaks.

"Think! You're just going through the motions,"

the coach shouted, a bib of sweat clinging to the front of his sweatshirt. Lincoln looked at James, who had scored five buckets, his best performance this year. James wiped his face with his arm and popped his knuckles one by one.

In the second half the A-team pulled away in spite of James's one-man show of four more buckets. Lincoln scored only three buckets during that half, and he trudged up the floor, toe hurting.

Coach grew tired of running up and down the court, yelling. He threw himself into a folding chair and only now and then shouted "Foul!" or "Get in his face!"

At the end of the fourth period, the score was 47–32. Coach made the boys do three laps around the gym before he let them shower. On the last lap, Coach joined them and tried to be jolly, but the teams just looked at the floor, breathing hard. The cheerleaders were gone. The shafts of sunlight that had blazed on the gym floor were gone. The heater was off, and the janitor was pulling the windows shut.

In the shower, James bragged about scoring eighteen points.

"Seriously, Linc, I'm for real. I can hit outside or inside. I can snake through the smallest gap. Hey, I like that. Snake. 'Snake James.'"

"Right, homes," Lincoln said, moving so that the machine-gun burst of water bounced against his chest. He had to agree that James had played a scrappy game. The little guy could leap like a trout, claw like a bear. "You did all right. Let me use your shampoo."

James threw him the tube. Lincoln squeezed it until a coil of blue stuff dribbled onto his palm.

"How's the toe?"

"Hurts. Coach is on my back."

"Yeah, he can be weird."

A crown of suds grew tall and white on Lincoln's head. He faced away from the shower, and the hot water cut hard into his back.

By the time Lincoln and James finished showering, dusk had settled in the streets. The billboard across from school was lit, advertising a soft drink by showing two guys on a surfboard. At the corner, cars idled at a red light, the ghosts of white exhaust blowing from their tailpipes and rising into the dark air.

Lincoln wondered about surfing, a *gavacho* pastime. What he knew was the indoor pool at Mission Community Center and a thousand brown bodies kicking the water white.

They walked in silence, each exhausted from hard play. James pinched a few Cornnuts from a pocket of his jacket and popped them into his mouth. James asked, "What do you think of Monica? Pretty cute, huh?"

Lincoln searched the corners of his own jacket for Cornnuts, sunflower seeds, a flake of a potato chip— anything to replace the salt he'd left on the gym floor. "She's *real* cute. Do you have any more Cornnuts?"

"Yeah."

"Do you think she has a boyfriend?" Lincoln asked as he ground the Cornnut to mush between his teeth.

"No."

"What makes you say no?"

"I don't know. She doesn't seem the type."

They walked in silence for two blocks before Lincoln asked, "What kind of type is she?"

"You know, the kind that studies. Pretty straight. Good at math."

Lincoln thought of Vicky, his ex-girlfriend. She was smart, too, but she was different from Monica, maybe a little taller, maybe more social. But he couldn't say for sure. Both were Mexican-American and cute, but at this point neither was part of his life.

They stopped at the 7-Eleven and bought another bag of Cornnuts and a Slurpee, which they shared, lapping up the sweetness of cherry-flavored ice. Lincoln licked the salty Cornnuts from his palm.

Lincoln told James he had to get home to start dinner. There were potatoes to peel, and Flaco would need company. Before he got hurt, Flaco had spent his days roaming about sniffing the lawns of the new neighborhood. But now Flaco stayed around the porch and the backyard and slept under the pear tree, unnoticed by the neighbor's cat, who sometimes climbed over the fence to eat from his bowl.

As Lincoln turned onto his block, their neighbor to the north, Mr. Schulman, was pulling his Mercedes into his driveway. Lincoln said "hi" as he passed Mr. Schulman, who was getting out of his car with a bulging briefcase, his arm pinching a large black book against his chest. The neighbor said "hello" and turned away in a fit of coughing. His belly wiggled over his belt, and even in the half-darkness, Lincoln could see that Mr. Schulman was not a happy man.

Flaco was sitting on the front lawn. When he heard Lincoln's footsteps, he beat his tail against the grass and tried to walk despite his bandaged front leg. Lincoln hugged his dog and ran a hand through his dusty fur. He pulled out a leaf caught in his collar and said, "My foot hurts, too. You gotta hang, my man."

The dog had been a gift from Lincoln's father when he and his mother separated. Lincoln had been seven, and he had cried when his father left the house with a small TV and boxes of clothes. He saw his father now and then, but mostly his contact with him was through letters and birthday cards thick with one-dollar bills. Once his father had sent him a pair of boxing gloves, which he and Tony had laced up to beat each other silly for two hours straight. But that was years ago. His father was now living in Los Angeles, and Lincoln and his mother were in northern California, in a dull suburb that went to sleep at nine o'clock sharp.

Together Flaco and Lincoln walked up the steps, slow because of Flaco's bandaged leg, and went in the front door.

The steam of cooking beans and potatoes uncurled into the air, fogging up the windows.

Lincoln threw his backpack on the couch and called out, "Hi, Mom. You home early?"

"I'm in here." His mother was in the kitchen, pounding a round steak with a knife he had bought for her birthday. He realized a knife was not a sentimental gift, but he liked the way it looked, with a black handle and a dime-bright blade so sharp it could split a hair nine ways—or so he imagined.

"I was done with work—*cansada*," she said. She was in a jogging suit. Her hair was tied back in a bandanna, and her feet were smothered in the rabbit slippers he had bought her last Christmas. "*Mi'jo*, Tony called. He wants you to call back."

Lincoln turned down the radio, which was playing Marvin Gaye's "I Heard It Through the Grapevine."

"What did he want? I forgot to remind him this morning he still owes me two dollars."

"*No sé. Llámalo.* Why does he owe you two dollars?"

The oven door squeaked open, and his mother

brought out a large black frying pan that Lincoln always thought must be from Mexico. Lincoln had seen white people cook with chrome- or copper-colored fry pans, but every Mexican mother Lincoln knew cooked her groceries into savory delights in black cast-iron pans.

"It's an old bet. Remember when the 'Niners were playin', Mom?"

"No," she said.

"It was a bet on the game, and he never paid."

Lincoln went to the sink and got himself a tall glass of water. His mother noticed his limp and asked, "*¿Qué te pasó en la pierna?* What happened to your leg?"

He caught his breath after drinking long and hard and said, "It's my toe. I hurt it again in practice."

"You should soak it. And rest. I got us a video for tonight. *The Birds.*"

"I saw it. But I'll see it again." Lincoln got another glass of water and this time drank slowly. Out of the corner of his eye, he saw Flaco pawing the pantry door.

"*¿Tienes hambre?*" Lincoln asked as he bent down on one knee and took Flaco's head into his hands. He ruffled Flaco's fur and combed it with his hand. "Mom, what's the word for 'dog food' in Spanish?"

His mother stopped and looked at the wall, brow pinched in thought. "*No sé.* Ask your Spanish teacher."

Lincoln opened a can of dog food and scooped it out with a spoon. As he sat down in a chair to watch Flaco eat, he realized how tired he was. His toe throbbed. His wrist, slapped by Durkins in the first period, was bruised, and his arm hurt from when he caught an elbow while working inside under the hoop. He decided to take his mom's suggestion and soak his foot. As the bathtub filled with water, he decided to soak his whole body. He threw in handfuls of bubble bath and laughed as the pink suds grew mountainous.

"I deserve this," he said to himself as he lowered his body into the water. "Aah, it's hot."

While he rested in the water, steam rising like smoke from incense, he read the sports section of the newspaper. The Warriors had lost again. But they were the team to stand by. The Lakers, good as they were, with players like Magic Johnson and the spirit of the recently departed Kareem Abdul Jabbar, were to be hissed at. The Warriors, he thought, were like his old school, Franklin. Franklin was a poor school, grim and sad because the kids were poor—but scrappy, like the Warriors. The Lakers were like his new school, rich and full of the right moves.

Lincoln was drying off when he heard his mother say, "¡Ándale, muchacho! ¡Apúrate! Y sacá al Flaco. And take Flaco outside."

Lincoln scrubbed his hair dry with a towel and stepped back into his jeans. He put on a fresh T-shirt that read "Hey" and, barefoot, hurried to the kitchen. He tugged Flaco by the collar, put him out, and said, "Come on, chamaco."

Mother and son ate in silence. They were tired and hungry, and talking would keep them from slicing through steamy carne asada and scooping up frijoles and papas in rips of warm tortilla. His milk went down cold. His mother sipped from her glass of water. When Lincoln finished his first helping he said, "Ah, Mom, that was good," then helped himself to a second serving of frijoles and another tortilla.

Only when they were finished did they let Flaco

back in. Flaco dragged his leg and whined for a small taste of their dinner.

"¿*Qué quieres?*" Lincoln whispered when his mother got up to answer the telephone in the hall. He snatched a flag of meat from the pan, and Flaco leapt for it, hurt leg and all.

His mother returned to the kitchen. "¡*Ay Díos, que gente!* These people! They think money grows on trees. You give once to a charity, and now everyone calls."

Almost every evening some group—the Democratic Party, the Veterans of Foreign Wars, schools for the handicapped—called asking for money.

"It's because we live in a better part of town now."

"*A lo mejor.* Maybe."

The phone rang again, and this time it was his mom's new boyfriend, Roy. Lincoln listened to his mother say, "Yes, sounds good. No, you're silly. So we'll go out Friday. With Lincoln?"

Flaco looked at Lincoln, and Lincoln looked at the wall. He didn't like it when his mother dated men who flinched when a dog barked. And Flaco barked a lot.

After Lincoln washed the dishes he pushed in the videocassette, and they sat together on the couch, his mother with a cup of coffee, Lincoln with an ice cream drumstick, and Flaco with a Milk Bone.

Chapter

Lincoln woke to Flaco scratching the front door. His mother was in the bathroom using the hair dryer.

"Mom," Lincoln hollered sleepily. "Flaco wants in."

Flaco scratched and whined as the hair dryer wailed. Lincoln thought he heard eggs clacking in a pot of boiling water.

He lay in bed, eyes closed. It was Friday. There would be no basketball practice today. He wiggled his toe. It still hurt. His wrist was tender, and his shoulder pained him. He yawned and rolled onto his side.

As he lay in bed he thought of the gym at his old school; three banners from the championship years 1967, 1970, and 1977 hung near the rafters, faded and dusty with neglect. Those years were before his time, before anyone's time. It seemed so long ago.

He thought about Monica. Was she getting up from bed? Was she combing her hair in front of the bathroom mirror? Was she at the breakfast table, dabbing a piece of tortilla into yellow egg yolks? He wondered if she spoke in Spanish or English to her parents. Lately, he and his mother had started using English, even at home. Lincoln's Spanish was getting worse and worse.

When he heard his mother call, he rolled onto his stomach and pushed himself up quickly, letting his blankets slip onto the floor. He shivered and said, "*Ay, hace mucho frio,*" and pulled on a sweater, backward, over his pajama top. He felt the label tickle his chin, but he didn't bother to fix it.

He shuffled to the kitchen, where his mom, pink from showering, was putting bread into the toaster. He was right: soft-boiled eggs and toast with a smear of jam.

"I'm gonna let Flaco in," he said as he passed her and went into the living room.

Flaco's nose was pressed to the window, and when he saw Lincoln he barked loudly.

"*Ya, perrito,*" Lincoln called, hurrying over the cold floor.

Flaco nudged his body through the door and, without even glancing up at Lincoln, hobbled to his bowl.

At the breakfast table, his mother said that Roy, her boyfriend, would be coming over that night. The three of them might go out for dinner.

"Do I have to?" Lincoln asked. He didn't like Roy, who was shorter than his mother. He drove a baby-blue BMW—a girl's color, Lincoln thought—and was, like Mr. Schulman, pudgy and pale. Lincoln figured he couldn't run around the block without stopping to pinch the pain in his side. Some man.

"It'd be nice," his mother said. "He likes you."

Lincoln chewed his toast but didn't say anything. For a second he thought of his father, but when he couldn't picture what he looked like he thought of the creaking rafters of his old gym—those three banners, limp and faded and nearly forgotten.

Without thinking, Lincoln asked, "What's Dad doing? We never hear from him."

His mother chewed slowly and, after clearing her throat, said, "He's still in Los Angeles. He's still a parole board officer."

"What's that?"

"You know. He works for the police department. He checks up on criminals when they get out of prison. It's a hard job."

"Do I look like him?"

His mother smiled and touched his hair. "You're just like him. Strong."

Lincoln didn't want to think about his father, and he didn't want to think about Roy. He cracked open his geography book, and once again it fell open to the page of the camel driver with the broken teeth and lined face. It was a hard life for him, too, and for everybody who worked under the sun.

"I have to hurry," Lincoln said, taking his plate to the sink.

"Then you'll come with us?" she asked.

"We might have late practice," he lied. There never was practice on Friday. Coach Yesutis belonged to a bowling league, and Friday was their night to play.

He could feel his mother staring at him as he walked to his bedroom. He dressed quickly, combed his hair and brushed his teeth, and was out the door before his mother could kiss him. He barely heard her say, "Have fun at school."

Lincoln caught up with James, and since they were early they stopped at the 7-Eleven for an apple pie, which they tore in half and wolfed down. They licked their fingers, and James said, "Man, that was good."

They walked in silence. Then Lincoln asked, "What does your dad do?"

"He's a surveyor."

"A surveyor?" Lincoln asked, surprised. He had expected to hear "a doctor" or "a lawyer." Everyone in Sycamore seemed to have a fancy job.

"Yeah, that's his racket. He's one of those guys you

see standing in an orange vest by the freeway." James picked up a rock and hurled it at a sparrow on a telephone wire. "Mom's the one who makes the big bucks. She has an import store in Burlingame. Some of the stuff is from Mexico."

Lincoln kicked a pile of leaves and tried to remember if he had seen her store. His uncle Raymond lived in Burlingame, and Lincoln had spent a week there after his father and mother had gotten their divorce.

They got to school a few minutes before the tardy bell rang. Mr. Kimball, his hair messy from a wind that was hauling in dark storm clouds, was waiting with his tardy slips.

"Not today, Mr. Kimball," James mouthed off.

"But I'll get you," Mr. Kimball answered back. He chuckled under his breath.

Lincoln and James smiled as they hurried past him to first period. Lincoln couldn't concentrate on algebra. Basketball was on his mind. He closed his eyes and faces flashed before him—his ex-girlfriend, Vicky; Monica Torres; Roy in his baby-blue BMW; his mother; Coach Yesutis yelling on the sidelines. An image of Vicky, snapping a mouthful of Juicy Fruit gum, asked with a sneer, "What side ya on?"

"Mendoza, answer this problem," Mr. Green called out, and Vicky's image burst like a soap bubble. He was pointing to a problem on the board.

Lincoln looked up, startled. "Ah, well, it's—ah, let me see, it's . . . whatever you say."

A few students turned to look at him. Durkins, the forward on the second-string team, grinned at him. He wouldn't have known the answer either.

Mr. Green wet his lips and, behind the glint of thick glasses, stared at him, hard. Lincoln, feeling like an idiot, looked down at his hands folded on his desk, which was scarred with the initials "C. O." Lincoln traced his fingers over the letters, sorry that he couldn't answer Mr. Green.

Rain was coming down hard by the time the bell rang and algebra class let out. Lincoln shouldered his backpack. As he passed the teacher he muttered, "I'm sorry." Mr. Green, shuffling a batch of papers, said, "Your grades are slipping. What's wrong?"

"Nothin'."

"Are you sure?"

"I'll try harder," Lincoln said, and turned away. Then he turned back to say, "This school's different," and left without explaining what he meant.

In spite of his hurt toe, he ran to his history class, where he learned that chickens came to Egypt from India.

Man, that was a long walk, Lincoln thought. He smiled as he pictured hordes of white-throated chickens clucking over sand dunes and taking boats up the Nile to Alexandria.

"Were they chickens like today's chickens?" Andy, the A-plus-in-everything-but-P.E. student, asked. His pen was poised and ready for Mrs. Wade, the teacher, to answer.

"No one knows," she replied.

That's a good answer, Lincoln thought. It seems like we can't remember last week. How are we gonna remember way back then?

By lunch period, the rain had stopped and a slice of blue showed above the school. Lincoln ate his lunch standing under a tree. He bit three times into a bruised apple and pitched it into the trash can—two points, he thought—then went looking for Monica Torres. He wanted to see her, to talk with her. His heart thumped like a basketball bouncing down stairs.

"What am I gonna say to her?" he muttered to himself. He looked in the cafeteria, but she wasn't there amid the din of forks dropping and students laughing and yelling. He walked between the lockers. He went into the gym, where three girls were huddled together talking. But she wasn't there. Finally, he found her in the library, writing in what he figured was her journal for English.

He walked up to her and said, "Hi."

"Oh, hello, Lincoln," she replied. "Where's James?"

"I don't know," he answered, pulling out a chair and sitting down. The librarian looked his way, and he gave her a nod. "Eating lunch, I guess." He peeked at her journal and asked, "Whatta you writin'?"

She closed her journal and after a moment of silence said, "Oh, just about last night."

"What happened last night?"

She turned over an eraser between her fingers and said she had had an argument with her father. "I told my dad that I wanted to quit aikido, but he got mad and said I was spoiled. He said that when he was a kid he worked in the fields—" She stopped suddenly.

"Yeah, I know the rap. My mom did her share of field work in the Valley." He took the eraser away from her and squeezed it until his knuckles turned bone white. "Yeah, every Christmas when we go down to Fresno—that's where *mi familia* is—they talk about cardboard in their shoes. Blisters. Lawn-mowing jobs. It's boring."

"My dad's from Salinas. He used to cut broccoli and artichokes. I don't like broccoli, do you?"

"It's all right. Brussels sprouts are my problem."

"Brussels sprouts," Monica mused. "That's another one I can't stand."

Lincoln looked up at the clock on the wall. It was five minutes to one. I had better make my move, he thought to himself. His heart did it again.

"Monica, I was wondering, uh," Lincoln began, biting his lip. "I was thinking maybe we can . . . I don't know, maybe shoot some hoop this Saturday?"

"Saturday? I can't," she answered, smiling and stuffing her binder into her backpack. "I'm going somewhere."

The basketball in his heart went flat.

Then she added, "But how about Sunday? Late afternoon, maybe three o'clock?"

The basketball filled with air and went bumping down the stairs, out of control.

"Yeah!" he cried. "Sounds fine! Where?"

The librarian looked at him and pursed her lips.

Monica, slinging her backpack onto her shoulder, said, "Cornell Elementary. That's where I slam and dunk."

"'Slam and dunk'—I like that." Lincoln couldn't believe his good fortune. She talks like a guy, but she's so cute, he thought.

Lincoln walked to class in a daze. After school he hurried home, nearly running in spite of his hurt toe and the weight of weekend homework on his shoulders. Not to mention worry about Roy.

Chapter 5

The bus rumbled from the slick commercial streets of the suburbs to the litter-blown barrio of Lincoln's childhood. When he first boarded the bus, the few passengers, almost all of them retired people with carts for Saturday shopping, spoke English. But after twenty stops, after trim houses gave way to apartment buildings and poorly kept muffler and tire shops, the bus filled with brown-faced *raza*. English gave way to singsong Spanish. Almost every woman had a child.

"*¡Ándale, muchacho!*" a mother scolded her boy affectionately as he unhooked the Pepsi cans that he had smashed onto his shoes. The boy laughed and waved good-bye to the cans as his mother yanked him onto the bus. She dropped coins into the box and took a transfer from the driver, a black man in sunglasses clear enough to show his eyes. She muttered, "*Con permiso, con permiso,*" as they made their way to a seat near the exit.

The woman smiled at Lincoln, a gold cap gleaming on her front tooth, and said loud enough for everyone to hear, "*Mi hijo es un diablito.* My son's a little devil." She patted her lap, and the boy leaped onto it. The boy turned and smiled at Lincoln, who nearly jumped because the boy's front teeth were gone. He reminded Lincoln of himself when Tony had kicked his front teeth out going down the slide.

Lincoln thought of Tony. He had called early that morning, while Lincoln was still in bed curled into the warmth of his blankets. Tony's voice had seemed urgent.

"Linc, you got to get down here," he had said.

"What's up?"

"I can't tell you why, *ese.* You gotta see for yourself."

"You owe me two bucks, Tony. Remember the 'Niners game?"

"Yeah, yeah. I'll pay you, but you gotta check this out."

So Lincoln had boarded a nearly empty bus that slowly filled with brown people, while his mother had breakfast with Roy. Last night it was Thai food with Roy, and this morning, eggs Benedict at a fancy restaurant in Palo Alto. Last night Lincoln had told his mom that his toe hurt, and he wanted to watch a video and suck up a bowl of Top Ramen noodles with Flaco at his side. This morning he told her he wanted to see Tony, to kick around the Mission District.

Lincoln stared out the window. He saw a dog carrying a fan belt in his mouth. He saw a kid burst a light bulb against the ground, his hands pressed to his ears. He saw a man with a shopping cart brimming with crushed aluminum cans. He recalled the Pepsi cans the little boy had left in the gutter. He looked over to the mother and boy, but they were gone. A *vato loco* sat in their place, a knee going up and down to the rhythm inside his head. A tattooed cross darkened his wrist.

Lincoln got off the bus and walked toward Tony's house on Day Street. A man with sores on his face the color of crisp bacon asked for a handout, but Lincoln shook his head and looked down as he walked by.

"You'll know 'bout it one day," the man muttered.

Lincoln felt bad, but if he gave the man a dollar, he would have no way to get home. And anyway, how could a dollar change that man's life and wipe those sores off his face?

Lincoln stopped in front of *Discolandia* and searched the window display for a record for his mother. Her birthday was coming up, and she had hinted for an album by *El Chicano*. He cupped his hands over his eyes and looked. But what caught his attention were three men in the back. They were playing cards, poker, Lincoln figured. The tips of their cigarettes glowed.

Lincoln stepped back and looked at his watch. It was 9:30. He continued walking in the direction of Tony's house. He was happy to be in the old neighborhood.

Tony answered the door on the first knock. He was dressed in sweats, with gym shorts on the outside. His sweatshirt had a Champion spark plug on the front, and his Giants baseball cap was turned backwards.

"Linc, *no hables fuerte*. Don't talk so loud. Mom's on the phone."

"I didn't say anything," Lincoln whispered as he walked into the house. "Who's on the phone?"

"Some dummy's trying to sell her encyclopedias, but she is saying that she got no kids."

That's weird, Lincoln thought. Telephone salesmen were hitting on poor people, too. He had thought it just happened in his new neighborhood.

They tiptoed down the narrow hallway, the wooden floor squeaking. Lincoln looked at Tony's three younger brothers, all sitting on the couch watching Saturday morning cartoons with the sound turned down. They waved to Lincoln and smiled so that the red licorice whips they were chomping on showed between their teeth. The littlest one put a finger to his lips and said loudly, "Linc, don't make no noise. Mama's on the phone."

Everyone hushed him, and his hand went to his mouth as he muffled a giggle.

"Why don't your mom just hang up?" Lincoln asked.

"Mom's too nice. She should tell the guy to get lost."

The two of them went into the kitchen, where Tony's mother was ironing a shirt and saying into the telephone, "I got a lot of books, young man. And the library is down the street, not far. It's open all the time." Her hair was piled with blue curlers, and her forehead was smeared with white beauty cream.

He had known Mrs. Contreras as long as he could remember, before he could count to ten and tie his shoelaces, before he could pedal a bike without training wheels, before his father left and took a job in another town.

She looked up, and her eyes sparkled at Lincoln. She blew him a kiss with her fingertips and said into the telephone, "I gotta go. But nice books. You're nice, too."

She placed the receiver down and her face broadened with a smile.

"Ay, mi'jo. Qué grande te has puesto. How tall you've gotten. Whatta you eatin' at home?" she said as she patted the curlers on top of her head. "Qué guapo estas. How handsome you are. How's your mother? She never calls or nothin'."

She turned off the iron and gave him un abrazo that nearly took his breath away and popped out his eyeballs.

"Hello, Mrs. Contreras," he said. He wiped his cheek where some of her beauty cream had rubbed off on him.

"Hello yourself, *mi hombrecito*. Look, you're taller than Tony."

"Mama, he was always taller," Tony said. He picked up an apple from the table and bit into it.

"*Pues no*. When you two were little babies, you were taller."

"Really?" Tony responded.

"I stretched you both out on the grass one day. *Tu estaba mas grande y mas gordo*. You were bigger and fatter."

"On the grass?" Tony asked.

"*Sí. Hacía calor y* you babies were sweatin' and crying. I put you on the grass and turned the hose on you."

"The hose?" they both asked, nearly screaming.

"To cool you babies."

Tony gagged on a mouthful of apple. He glanced at Lincoln with a look that said "*qué loca*."

"*¿Mi'jo, tienes hambre?*" she asked Lincoln as she folded the ironing board and leaned it against the wall.

"No, I'm not hungry. But can I have a glass of water?"

"*Claro*," she said, feeling the curlers. She started toward the faucet but stopped. "*No, no, les voy hacer una limonada*."

While Mrs. Contreras swirled lemonade from a can into a pitcher painted with the faces of the San Francisco Giants, Tony pulled Lincoln into his messy bedroom. A pile of clothes lay in the corner, dark with dirt and streaks of grass stains. A cracked Raiders football helmet was propped on a bedpost.

His chest of drawers gleamed with baseball and basketball trophies that belonged to him and his older brother, Fausto, who was away at college.

Tony tossed the apple onto the chest. "Linc, you know when your house was ripped off?"

"What about it?"

Tony closed the door. "Dig this—I know where the TV is!"

Lincoln knitted his brow. He picked up a baseball from the floor and scratched at the already ripped seams. "*Chale*," he said, incredulous. "Are you making it up?"

Tony picked up his pajamas from the floor. "*No, es en serio*. You know that thrift shop on Dolores near the church? A *viejo* runs the place."

Lincoln had passed the thrift store a hundred times on his way to and from Franklin. He had even bought his mother a swivel lamp there for her birthday. "You jivin' me?"

Tony assured him he wasn't. He had been in there yesterday looking for forks.

"Forks?" Lincoln asked. "That's weird."

"They're for Mom. We lost a bunch, the ones Dad got her for Christmas from the Price Club. Fausto took them away to college. He didn't even ask Mom. The jerk."

Lincoln let the baseball roll out of his palm, and it raced under Tony's bed like a mouse. In his mind he could see his TV sitting among the piles of old records, clothes, busted toys, chipped plates and cups, and scuffed shoes that stank of asphalt and dead grass. He could see the owner sitting in his La-Z-Boy recliner, his bifocals on the bridge of his veined nose, his hands peppered with age.

"You sure it's *my* TV?" Lincoln asked.

"*Sí, hombre*. It's the one with crayon marks, ain't it?"

"Crayons?"

Then Lincoln remembered how, when he was eight, he'd colored the side of the television for fun. Fun that got him a spanking from his mother and a week without television.

With the heel of her palm, Tony's mother pounded on the door and yelled, "*Muchachos*, boys, come and drink your *limonada*. And I fixed us some popcorn."

"*Bueno,* Mama," Tony said. They left the bedroom thinking of the TV.

After a glass of lemonade with ice cubes, some fistfuls of popcorn, and some talk with Tony's mother, who propped her large dimpled elbows on the table, the two of them put on their jackets and headed for the thrift shop. Lincoln had to see for himself.

Chapter 6

Lincoln and Tony walked in step, hands curled into fists and pushed deep into their pockets. The wind had shoved the morning clouds east. The day was finally warming.

"So how we gonna get back the TV?" Tony asked.

They leaped over a garden hose. A guy in a 49ers jacket was hosing down his car for a Saturday wash and polish. His baby son was squeezing a dry sponge and giggling.

"I don't know. Let's be cool and say we're lookin' around."

"Forks. I can tell the *viejo* that I'm still lookin' for forks."

In his mind, Lincoln pictured Tony's brother skipping town with a pocketful of Mrs. Contreras's dinnerware. "OK, that might work. But let's not jump on the dude."

"*¿Y por qué no?* He's got your TV, doesn't he?"

"Maybe someone sold it to him. Maybe he found it."

"Aw, man, where's he gonna find a TV? Did he walk down the street, spot one in an alley, and say, 'Hey look, I found a free TV'? Wake up, Linc. This guy's a crook. You been livin' with white folks too long."

Lincoln stopped and snapped, "*¡Chale!* Don't tell me that! You know where I come from. I come from *here*." He pointed to the street, and the street looked grim with busted glass and a smashed battery in the gutter, junky cars, a drunk sipping from a bottle in a paper bag, scruffy dogs, and metal-flake Chevys purring at the red light.

"I don't mean it like that," Tony replied, his voice going soft. "You know, people change."

Lincoln stared at his friend angrily. "Not me. I'm brown, not white. *Y que no se te olvide.* And don't you forget it." Lincoln looked away. Across the street a man was pushing a shopping cart overflowing with empty soda cans.

"I didn't mean it like—"

"Let's not talk about it. Things change, but people stay the same."

They continued walking more slowly, their hands now at their sides. For two blocks they didn't say anything. Lincoln wondered if he had changed like Tony said. Sycamore was soft and lazy, and his school was all white, or nearly all white—except for a couple of black kids and a knot of Koreans who sat by themselves at lunchtime. His new friends from Sycamore probably ate Brie on stone-ground crackers, not like his *gente,* who chomped into *queso* melted inside tortillas. Where he came from, you threw punches if someone accidentally bumped against you. Where he lived now, you just walked away. You wouldn't want to mess up your clothes.

They stopped to buy gum, sunflower seeds, and a Coke, which they shared. They were in a better mood when they arrived at the thrift shop, which was small and run-down. The front window was dirty and fly-specked. In one corner, a cardboard sign read: Clean Goods for a Good Price.

A woman was leaving, a bag clutched under her arm. She was Mexican, and when she passed, Lincoln and Tony said, "*Buenos días, señora.*" They stared at her until she rounded the corner.

They turned their attention back to the thrift store. They circled outside, unsure about what to do, kicking the gutter with the tips of their sneakers and biding their time. Tony, cupping his hands around his eyes, peeked in the front window. The owner was in his La-Z-Boy recliner, seemingly asleep. Tony turned to Lincoln, who was leaning against a parked car, and suggested, "Let's just go in and look around. It's no crime."

"*Espérate.*"

Tony shrugged his shoulders and looked down at the sidewalk, where a dime gleamed. He bent down and picked it up, turning it over and scratching off the beard of grime that hung on Roosevelt's face. "Here, Linc. Here's part of what I owe you on our bet." He held up the dime and grinned.

"Keep it. I want my money in full. Crisp dollars, not chump change you find on the ground."

"Only kiddin'. I got the money at home." Tony flipped the coin and slapped it between his palms. "Whatta you say, heads or tails?"

Lincoln thought a moment, then said, "Heads."

Tony peeked between the sandwich of his palms, and a slow grin broke out across his face. "Sorry, Charlie, it's tails."

"But we didn't bet," Lincoln protested.

"OK, then, this is for reals. Double or nothin' on our 49ers bet."

Lincoln bit a fingernail, spit its paring, and agreed. "But you better pay me."

Smiling so that his chewing gum showed, Tony flipped the coin and slapped it from the air onto the back of his hand this time. "Whatta you say?"

"Heads."

Lincoln and Tony peeked, full of anticipation. It was heads. Tony jumped back and hollered, "¡*Chale!* You got me."

"Four bucks," Lincoln said, rubbing his palms together.

Tony turned away, grumbling. He looked back into the thrift store, where the old man still slept in the recliner. Tony stepped back and, admiring his reflection in the window, slicked down his hair. He smiled and his teeth, which were as large as guitar picks, glowed white against his brown face.

Lincoln pushed himself off the car's fender. "Let's get it done. But don't jump on the dude."

Lincoln really didn't care about the TV, but he was still upset about someone breaking into his house. If that hadn't happened, perhaps they would still be living in his old neighborhood. He would be playing for Franklin, not Columbus, and life would be sweet. He would still be with Vicky, and Flaco would never have gotten hit by a motorcycle.

A tiny bell hooked on the door jingled as they entered. A yellow canary beat its wings in a cage and squawked. The old man, running a pink tongue over his whiskered upper lip, slowly turned his large head toward them. His eyes were watery. His teeth were stained and broken like jagged pieces of pottery. He wore a pair of gardening gloves splotched with white paint.

"May I help you?" the man asked as he pushed himself up from the recliner and sneezed. A gust from the opening and closing of the door hit him. "It's cold in here," he remarked.

The store smelled of shoe polish and old coats. Turpentine. Dust and mothballs. A calendar showing a New England waterfall scene was nailed to the wall. Its pages were yellow and curling.

"Forks," Tony responded.

"What?" the man asked. He touched his ear with a gloved finger. "My hearing's gone. What's that?"

"*Mi hermano* took off with the forks, man," Tony snapped. "How come you can't hear?"

Lincoln made a face at Tony and whispered, "Cut it out." He turned slowly to the man, who was now walking up an aisle to the cash register. "We're just looking around, sir."

With a shove of his good foot, Lincoln pushed a box of rain-warped *National Geographics* out of his way. Tony started to look around. He pulled on the chain of a lamp. "Don't work," he muttered. He pounded on a black typewriter and the gummed-up keys stuck as they rose up in surrender. "Don't work," he said again. He held up a Hawaiian shirt. "Whoever wore this was a fat dude. *Un gordo.*" Tony cocked a derby on his head and smiled into a mirror. "And check out this hat. Gramps musta worn this before you and me were born, Linc."

Lincoln told Tony to cut it out.

"This is a kick, *hombre*," Tony sounded off. "*Aliviánate.* Lighten up. Hey, look at these boxer shorts."

Lincoln ignored Tony, who was holding up a pair of candy-cane-striped boxers. Instead, he maneuvered around broken furniture to the TV. Tony tossed the boxers away and followed Lincoln, who tried the on and off button and played with the rabbit-ear antenna. He examined the crayon marks—an arc of rainbow colors—on the side of the television. He remembered that day clearly. He had been bored from three days of rain and without thinking used a pack of forty-eight Crayolas to make the television pretty—or so he later argued to his mother as she spanked him from one room to the next.

They looked at one another.

"*¿Qué te dije?*" Tony said. "What'd I tell you?"

"*Sí*, it's ours." Lincoln sighed. He snapped his chewing gum and looked at the old man. "*¿Qué piensas que debemos hacer?* What should we do?"

"Jack him up. Tell the old guy this is yours."

They turned around. The old man was stirring a teaspoon of instant coffee into a Disneyland mug. His gloves were off, and Lincoln could see that his hands were purple and shaking, the skin paper-thin. The old man looked up, and with an index finger he wiped a teary eye. He looked sick.

"Tony, how do you think he coulda stole the TV?"

"*¿Aquí la tiene, no?* It's here, ain't it?"

"*Sí*. It's here, but do you think he sneaks around during the day looking for houses to rip off? Come on, man. The dude's sick."

"*¿Linc, como lo sabes?* How do you know?"

Lincoln watched the old man sip his coffee through a puckered clot of whiskers. "He got the TV somehow, but I don't want to know how." He walked away from Tony and picked up two mismatched salt shakers. He pounded their bottoms and a few grains rained onto the floor.

"I know how," Tony said. He turned around and snapped, "Hey, *señor*, where did you get the TV? It ain't yours."

The old man touched his ear. "What?"

"I said, where did you get the TV?"

"You want the shakers?"

"No, man, get the wax out. I'm talkin' 'bout the TV."

Lincoln pulled on Tony's sleeve hard. "Leave him alone, I tol' you. I said I don't care 'bout the TV or nothin'."

Tony sneered at Lincoln and said, "You're getting soft, Linc. Just 'cause you live with white people."

Lincoln wanted to punch Tony, but instead he walked to the door, his hands doubled up into fists. He was mad at everything and everyone—his mom's new business, the dullness of his new neighborhood, Franklin, Columbus, and now even his *carnal,* Tony.

Lincoln had been taught that he should always treat older people with respect, even if they were wrong. And he didn't believe that the old man had stolen the TV. The guy could barely get out of his La-Z-Boy. How could he lift a TV onto his shoulder and saunter, whistling, out of a house in broad daylight? He probably picked it up for a couple of dollars at a yard sale.

Lincoln yanked open the door, scaring up a loud noise from the bell, and started up the street. Tony followed, shouting, "*Escúchame,* Linc. Listen up. I know the guy is on the take. I know . . ."

Without as much as a "Back off, *tonto,* before I smack you one," Lincoln waved Tony off and didn't look back. He kept walking and walking until Tony's footsteps faded and he was far from the thrift shop, far from Tony's house, and miles from his own house in Sycamore. He walked so far that he once again was standing in front of Franklin, hands deep in his lint-flecked pockets as he stared at the school, full of sadness. He had gone there for two years, had fights there, played games there, found his first girl there. The teachers, tough from teaching inner-city kids, were the best. When they slapped you with detention, you knew it was for your own good.

He breathed in the years gone by and climbed the fence in three grunting moves. He walked toward the administration building, through dank open-air hallways smacking of neglect and poor grades to where the lockers stood against the walls. He walked over to his old locker. It was scratched with initials, phone numbers, and lopsided hearts. He tried the combination: 3–7–17. He yanked on the lock, but it wouldn't open its thick jaw. He walked over to Vicky's locker. He tried hers—24–16–9—and the lock gave. Slowly, his heart thudding from excitement, he opened her locker. Inside, he found balled gym socks, a sweater, and a pile of books. He felt the sweater and he opened a book. The pages fell open to a camel driver with a lined face and broken teeth.

Can't get away from that dude, Lincoln thought as he closed the locker. He relished the thought that he and Vicky were reading the same geography book. It was like still being together, still side by side as they did their homework.

He drank from the fountain and played hoop with some little kids on an asphalt court. He let them win—three *chavalos* against one big one—then took a rattling bus back home to Sycamore.

Chapter 7

Lincoln woke Sunday morning to Flaco scratching at the door. He listened to the sounds of water dripping from the faucet in the kitchen and the wind tapping a branch of the eucalyptus tree against his bedroom window. Lincoln, clutching his blankets, yawned, clicked his tongue against the roof of his mouth, and whispered sleepily, "What an ugly dream." In his dream, a black bear had tracked him through miles of slippery snow and pinned him to a tree, where the bear licked a raw wound on Lincoln's leg.

Lincoln rolled over to the cool side of his pillow. He thought of Tony. He shouldn't have jumped on his buddy like he did. It wasn't cool. After all, Tony was trying to help out.

He raised his head and looked at the clock on his chest of drawers. It glowed 8:17. Slowly Lincoln got out of bed, pulled a sweater over his pajama top, and walked down the hallway into the kitchen, where his mother, in her bathrobe, was already at the table, Sunday paper spread out in front of her.

She sipped her coffee and asked, "Do you want some breakfast?"

"I guess," Lincoln responded without thinking.

"Well, do you or don't you?" There was an edge to her voice. She looked tired, with dark circles under her eyes.

Lincoln looked at his mother and asked, "What time did you get home last night?"

She put down her coffee cup hard and snapped,

"Let's get one thing straight. I'm the parent, you're the child. I give the orders, and you take them. *Ay, muchacho,* I'm not one of your punky friends."

"My friends aren't punks."

"They're punks, *y tú te estás portando ahorita como uno de ellos.* You're acting like one yourself."

Lincoln didn't feel like arguing. He was still sleepy and cold. He got up and went to the front door to let in Flaco, who had begun to whine and scratch at the screen door.

"Yeah, I'd like some breakfast," Lincoln said, plopping back into his chair.

"Yeah? Is that a way to ask? Punks sound like that." His mother folded the newspaper and went to open the refrigerator. *"¡Ven acá! Pronto!"*

Lincoln sighed, rose slowly, and went to the refrigerator with Flaco following.

"I bring home *esto, y esto, y esto.*" She pointed to a ham, milk, eggs, and beans. *"¿Ahora dime, tú que traes a casa?* Tell me, what do you bring home?"

When Flaco tried to grab the ham, Lincoln pulled his collar roughly and turned away, muttering, "All right, I'm not hungry. You eat your groceries."

"Don't you talk to me like that," she yelled, slamming the refrigerator door. *"¿Y quíen te piensas que eres?* Who do you think you are?"

Why do people keep asking me that? Lincoln wondered. First Coach Yesutis, now Mom. He walked down the hallway with Flaco limping at his side. "It's one of those mornings," he said to himself as he closed the bedroom door and climbed back into bed. Flaco circled a pile of clothes, yawned, and then settled on top of them, paws pressed together and eyes turned sadly on the bulky outline of Lincoln under the blankets.

Lincoln lay in bed with the blankets over his head. He breathed in the warmth. He wondered what Tony was doing. He was probably in bed, his face buried in his pillow, or perhaps he was getting ready to go to church. Lincoln winced at the thought of how he had treated his old buddy. He pushed his friend out of his mind. Behind closed eyes, Lincoln pictured the bear, its teeth yellow as candle flames, viciously licking his wound. What a weird dream, he thought, and went back to sleep.

When he woke, the house was silent. His mother was gone to Sunday Mass, Lincoln figured. His alarm clock glowed 12:15, and a winter wind was still beating branches against the window. Lincoln stretched and let out a loud yawn, which stirred Flaco, who, in turn, stretched and yawned, his tongue arcing up and out.

Lincoln wandered into the kitchen. He looked in the refrigerator but closed it when he remembered that these were his mother's groceries, not his. He drank a tall glass of water, dressed in his sweats, ran a comb through his hair, and left the house. He and Flaco took a walk up his street, which was quiet and empty as an abandoned bird's nest. He wasn't going to meet Monica at Cornell Elementary until three o'clock.

Lincoln tossed a stick and Flaco hobbled after it, his dirty bandage picking up more dirt. Lincoln tossed a rock at a flood of pigeons cooing on a lawn, and they broke skyward.

Lincoln stopped in front of James's house and called out, "Homes, homes, you home?" After a while, James came out, rubbing his hands together and complaining, "Man, it's cold. It's gonna rain." They both looked up beyond the network of trees that lined their street. The sky was gray, hard as stone.

"What's goin' on?" James asked. "Joggin'?"

"On my hurt foot? Naw. Just walking Flaco, or maybe it's the other way around." Lincoln wanted to tell him about the argument with his mother, but he decided to keep it to himself.

"Why don't you come in for a sec?" James offered. "My parents just got back from church. They're cutting me some chow—honest-to-goodness venison."

"What's venison?" Lincoln asked.

"Deer meat."

Lincoln shrugged his shoulders at Flaco and said, "Never had that before." He looked down at Flaco. "Keep cool outside, Flaco. I'll be back."

Flaco rolled his tongue around his mouth, beat his tail against the grass, and lay in a pile of leaves.

Lincoln followed James into the house, which was warm and filled with the smells of bread and meat. An aquarium bubbled on a coffee table. Aretha Franklin's "Respect" was playing on the radio in a far room.

"Mom? Daddy-o?" James called. He said to Lincoln, "He likes 'Daddy-o.' He thinks he's a hippie." James called again. "Daddy-o, I want you meet a friend. A real ace."

As they walked to the dining room, Lincoln could hear the clack of dishes and the scrape of chairs. Mr. Kaehler was letting out a ho-ho laugh. Lincoln's nostrils pulled in the terrific smells of food. James whispered, "We like to grub on Sundays. Actually, any day. Eatin' is their sport."

His parents, both of them large and round-faced, smiled happily at Lincoln. Both of them were holding glasses of orange soda.

"Dad, this is Lincoln. He plays for us."

James's father extended a hand, which Lincoln pumped up and down. Turning to James's mother, he pumped hers as well, and then sat down at the table.

"Please help yourself," Mrs. Kaehler said.

The dining-room table was loaded with macaroni salad, three cheeses, dips and potato chips, French rolls, pilaf, and a slab of what was described by Mr. Kaehler as venison flown in from the state of Oregon. Saliva flooded Lincoln's mouth. "Well, thank you, maybe just a little snack."

Lincoln began to load his plate while James's father asked him about basketball, school, his family, and how he thought the San Francisco 49ers would do in the playoffs. Mr. Kaehler wadded a napkin and tossed it toward a wastebasket. "I used to play ball. But mostly I do this nowadays," he said, and pushed a forkful of meat into his mouth.

Lincoln thought about asking James's father about surveying but was afraid that he might go on and on. So he turned to Mrs. Kaehler and said, "James says you own a store."

"With a partner," she answered, uncapping a new bottle of orange soda. "I import primarily from Asia, but now with the import taxes getting—"

"The 'Niners look good, even with Montana hurt," Mr. Kaehler remarked, and held out his glass for a refill of soda.

Lincoln answered yes to every question that was asked him. He bit into a French roll and tried the venison. He sipped a soda, chewed on celery, rolled an olive into his mouth, scraped dip onto a corn chip. He sucked in macaroni salad. He chomped on a pickle. Lincoln sighed for the good life and thought to himself, Man, these folks can grub. Then, thanking James's parents, he disappeared with James into the living room, where they continued to eat and played Nintendo.

"Nice folks," Lincoln said. He tore off a piece of French bread and dipped it into a red crab sauce. While they played, they talked about the upcoming game with Franklin.

"I figure I'll get to play," James said. "When we get far enough ahead, Coach will let me play. Snake James. We should beat them bad."

"Maybe," Lincoln said. "But I think it'll be closer this time."

"Whatta you mean, 'maybe'? They should be a pushover. We beat 'em bad last time."

"Well, they're probably better."

"We're better too, then."

"But Coach is too rough on us. He's hard to work with."

"He's makin' us strong."

"You don't coach by callin' players names. And sometimes I don't think he knows what he's doing. His plays are stupid. Wait until we run up against a black team. You'll see."

Lincoln pushed his plate aside, patting his stomach. "You know it's my old school. They were holding back last time. Remember, it wasn't a league match. Why bring out the big guns when it don't count?"

James worked the Nintendo controls frantically, his little man bouncing over blocks and enemies. Windows of TV light were reflected in his eyes, which were large and worried because he was about to lose. "Aw, man, I messed up. The suckers got me."

He threw the controls aside. Lincoln started a new game, and his little man's life was rubbed out within a minute. "I'm no good, homes. Mom won't let me have a Nintendo because she says it's violent. Do I look violent, homes?" He contorted his face into dark lines and punched James in the arm—hard. James, playacting, rolled onto the floor and snickered, "You're a problem child. You need counseling."

"That's good, James." Lincoln laughed as he rose to his feet. "I have to go." He wanted to tell James about seeing Monica later, but he decided against it. It wasn't any of James's business.

"Let me show you something before you leave," James said. He led Lincoln down the hallway to his bedroom, which was neat and smelled of pine needles. A single trophy stood on a shelf and a faded second-place ribbon for swimming hung on the wall. His shoes were paired and facing the wall.

James went into his closet and brought out a boomerang. It was nearly three feet long, lacquered, and hard as bone.

"It's *bad*," Lincoln said. "You ever use it?"

"Sometimes. I hit a squirrel with it once."

"Did it die?"

"I don't know. It climbed a tree halfway, dropped, and ran real funny into the bushes."

Lincoln turned the boomerang over in his hands, admiring its gleam and hard angle. He rapped it against his wrist and said, "Man, this would hurt."

"Do you wanna try it? We could go down to the canal."

Lincoln thought of Monica. "Naw, I have to go. Maybe later."

James's parents were still sitting at the table, now watching a football game on TV. Lincoln shook Mr. Kaehler's hand and thanked Mrs. Kaehler, saying she was a great cook.

"We'll be at the game Tuesday," Mr. Kaehler said

as he walked Lincoln to the door. "James said he's going to play."

Lincoln looked at James. "Maybe."

"I'll play," James said. "Coach said so."

They stood in the doorway inviting him to come back again. Lincoln waved, and about halfway down the block he bent to pull a leaf from Flaco's collar. Flaco smelled food on Lincoln's breath and licked his face, partly for love, but mostly for the taste of meat.

Chapter 8

When Lincoln returned home, his mother was still gone—her Nissan Maxima was not in the driveway. He slipped a cassette of Ice-T, his favorite rap singer, into his blaster and did a light workout of sit-ups and fingertip push-ups. Standing in front of the hall mirror, his T-shirt tied around his waist, he flexed his muscles, which were cut with shadows and shining with sweat. He thought, my dad looked like this, and he smiled.

He showered, brushed his teeth until the gums hurt, and at two-thirty left to meet Monica at Cornell Elementary. He spun his best basketball on the tip of his index finger. The basketball was a leather Rawlings that had been a gift from the principal at Franklin when Lincoln was voted Player of the Year and made All-City—the only Mexican-American player, smiling among the black and white dudes. As Lincoln walked up the street, Flaco followed. Lincoln turned and said, "Stay!" and Flaco limped back to the porch, ears sagging.

Lincoln was nervous. He liked Monica. He thought she was cute, and he couldn't believe his good fortune when she told him that she could shoot hoop. We'll play Around the World, maybe Horse, then finish up with one-on-one, he thought. His former girlfriend, Vicky, didn't care for basketball. One time he had tried to teach her, but she got a bloody nose when he passed the ball—lightly, he thought—and it slipped between her hands and smashed her in the face.

He passed James's house and thought, nice folks. He walked up the street, kicking through leaves, feeling good. As he got closer to Cornell, his heart began to thump. His armpits were wet from nervousness. He stopped in front of the school, breathed in the winter air full of leaves and chimney smoke, and jumped the fence. He walked across the field toward the basketball courts.

"Oh, man, she's really there," he whispered to himself. In his heart, he had expected, almost hoped, that she wouldn't be there. He bounced his basketball onto the court. What would they talk about? He thought that maybe he could tell her about the venison he had grubbed at James's house. She, in turn, would ask, "What's venison?" He would tell her that it was deer meat and then brag that he often ate exotic meats. He laughed to himself. It sounded dumb. The only meats he really knew were steak and bologna. Nine years of hauling bologna sandwiches to school.

"That's stupid," he muttered to himself. "We can't talk about venison. I'll just let my mouth go and see what happens."

He started jogging slowly, the ball tucked under his arm, a smile on his face.

"Hi," Lincoln said, figuring that was a good enough start.

"Hi, Lincoln," Monica said. Her face was red from the cold and her hair mussed from the wind. She dribbled her ball, a synthetic Rawlings, he noticed, and she jumped, lean as a deer, and shot. The ball swirled off the rim.

"Been here long?"

"Not really."

Lincoln did an easy lay-up. He dribbled, then came

in, jumped four feet out, and snapped his fingers when it bricked.

"Did you go to church today?" Monica asked.

She pushed her hair from her face with a wave of her hand. Lincoln thought she was beautiful. He noticed her ring was not on her finger.

"Yes, eight o'clock Mass," he lied. "I always go."

"Which church?" Monica asked at the free-throw line. She bounced the ball twice and took aim.

"Which church?" Lincoln repeated. He dribbled his ball and said, "Well, ah, the one near my house."

Monica's shot swished the net.

"Which one is that? I go to Saint Jerome's."

Lincoln tried to remember the church his mother went to. It was Saint something. He went in for a reverse lay-up. He turned to Monica and said, "Saint Jay. That's it."

"Never heard of a Saint Jay."

Lincoln felt foolish. He changed the subject as he approached the free-throw line. "Guess what I had today?"

"Beats me." She stopped dribbling and looked directly at Lincoln. Her face was red and happy.

"Venison."

"Venison? You mean *deer?*" she said, startled. She dribbled toward the boards and did a reverse lay-up just as Lincoln's ball reached the rim. The balls collided and flew off in opposite directions. As Monica ran after her ball, she asked, "How could you eat deer? They're *so* cute."

"Yeah, they are," Lincoln said, and he almost added that they tasted good, too, especially between slices of rye bread. "I went to a friend's house—you know, James—and that's what they were eating. I couldn't tell them no."

Lincoln decided to shut up about church and food and just play basketball. He said, "How 'bout 'Round the World?"

"OK. You go first."

"No, please, you go first."

"No, I said, you go first."

Lincoln dribbled the ball between his legs—he couldn't resist showing off—and sank a shot off the backboard. He advanced to the next spot, which was so easy he could do it with his eyes closed. At the third spot, he missed and chanced. He made that bucket and moved to the free-throw line, then to the top of the key, where he missed and said, "*Ni modo.*"

It was Monica's turn. The first bucket was a cinch. The next attempt she missed but cleared when she chanced. She moved to the third spot, then to the free-throw line, where she missed.

"Do you think I should try?" she asked, dribbling the ball.

"Sure," Lincoln said.

She chanced and missed again, sending her back to the start. "Aw, darn. It's all your fault."

"*My* fault?"

"Yeah, you told me to try."

Lincoln decided to miss from the top of the key. He didn't want to get so far ahead that she would be out of competition.

Monica started again and advanced to the top of the key, where she missed. Lincoln, bouncing his ball, his mind now focused, thought, I better make my move. He shot and missed, and when he chanced he missed the rim altogether. Smiling at Monica, he said, "Oops."

Monica made the shot from the top of the key, the toughest in Around the World, and the next shots were easy. Then she had to return from the end to the start, and she won because an embarrassed Lincoln couldn't get past the top of the key.

It began to sprinkle, shining the black asphalt court. Next they played Horse, and because Lincoln was a better shooter, he won with only an H-O.

The rain forced Monica to pull up the hood of her sweatshirt, the front of which read Cal Berkeley. She shivered and said, "Lincoln, the rain's ruining the game. I think I better go."

Lincoln didn't want to stop. They had only been shooting and playing for half an hour. He had waited all weekend for this moment, and now—rain.

"Let's play a quick game of Twenty-one, OK?"

Monica slapped dirt from her palms. "OK. But remember, I'm out of shape. Don't laugh at me if I'm awful."

Lincoln, dribbling the ball between his legs, smiled. "I won't. I'll go slow. You take out."

He passed the ball to Monica and was relieved it didn't pass through her hands and smash her in the face.

Monica took it out, dribbling left, then cutting right. She shot from six feet out but missed. Lincoln picked up the ball and circled to the top of the key before cutting slowly left and forcing a reverse lay-up.

"That's cool," Monica said.

Lincoln was enjoying himself. His face was flushed from the heat of play. He liked feeling hot, feeling sweat on his brow. He dribbled to the top of the key and tossed the ball to Monica when she said "check."

She passed it back, and he took three steps and shot. The ball came off the rim. Monica picked it up, cleared it, and worked her way under the basket. Lincoln, arms outstretched, hovered above her. When he moved back a step to give her room to shoot, she jumped and caught her head square under his chin, sending him falling onto his back.

"¡Ay!" he screamed. He lay on the asphalt with his leg folded under him. Monica dropped to her knees and asked worriedly, "What happened?"

Lincoln sat up, blinking tears from his eyes. He looked at his palms, which were scraped red from the asphalt. "I'm OK, I think. What's the score?"

"Linc, don't be crazy. You can't play anymore. You're hurt. And look at the rain."

Lincoln looked skyward and got a face full of cold rain, which was now coming down hard. The court was entirely slick and shiny.

"Just let me rest for a sec."

Monica rose to her feet, knees wet. "Lincoln, I think you better go home and get some help."

She helped him to his feet, which Lincoln liked. Her hand, cold as it was, was terrific to hold, and he told her so.

"Oh, Lincoln, you're silly," she said, blushing.

"Do you have a boyfriend?" He could smell her shampoo and perfume.

"No, I don't," she said.

"Do you want one?"

She looked across the court. Her basketball had rolled to the monkey bars, where two smaller kids were swinging. "I've got to go. I'll see you Monday. You sure you'll be all right?"

"Yeah, sure," Lincoln answered, rubbing his knee.

Monica ran to get her basketball. But as she started to leave, her face wet from the rain, she said, "I'll be there when we play Franklin. Who are you gonna root for?"

That was a good question. Lincoln wondered

which side he should take. He was once a homeboy from the Mission District, but now he was a homeboy living in the suburbs and eating venison with *gavachos*.

"When you get home, rest your foot." Monica waved and jumped the fence. He liked that as well, a girl who could jump fences. Lincoln hobbled home, the pain in his knee growing with each step. By the time he climbed his front steps, the knee was swollen and stiff.

Flaco licked Lincoln's hands, barked, and followed him into the house. Roy and his mother sat in the living room listening to music, glasses of wine in their hands.

"Lincoln," Roy said chummily.

"Hi, *hijo*," his mother said, looking up.

They set their glasses down and smiled at Lincoln, who said, "I messed up my knee."

They asked in unison, "What happened?"

"I scrubbed at the courts." Lincoln sat down on the couch and rolled up his sweats. The knee was purple as an onion. "Man, it hurts. Hurts more than when I messed up my toe. I probably won't get to play Franklin."

"Beatrice, you'd better get some ice," Roy said, his face full of worry. "He needs to ice it down, then soak it." He turned to Lincoln and asked, "How did you fall?"

"Slipped. It's rainin'."

Roy said, "You know, I didn't tell you earlier, but I played for Franklin."

Lincoln, caught off guard, turned his attention from his knee to Roy. Roy seemed to be the furthest thing from a jock, even a junior-high jock. "You did?"

"Yeah. Back in 1970. I played forward. I wasn't

first-string, but I did get in there to throw my elbows around. In fact, I played against your coach, what's his name?"

"Coach Yesutis."

"Yeah, him." Roy sipped from his glass thoughtfully and said, "Yeah, he was a real punk."

"Coach Yesutis?"

"Yeah. He played for Columbus, your new school. I remember a game when he got fouled by one of our guys and yelled 'spic.' The whole school hissed him. We were playing on our turf, and we were mostly Mexican. I was the only white guy."

Lincoln's mother returned to the living room with a washcloth bulging with ice cubes. She placed it on his knee and asked, "What are you guys talking about?"

When they said "Basketball," she sat on the couch and picked up a magazine.

Roy turned his attention back to Lincoln. "Anyhow, one of our guys, Frankie Pineda, who was a real badmouth, pushed Yesutis, and Yesutis was stupid enough to push back. That's when the fireworks happened." Roy adjusted the ice pack on Lincoln's knee. "Frankie busted him in the face, and some guy even came down from the bleachers to smack Yesutis. I think Frankie got kicked out of school for a week."

"Man, that's sorry. Did Yesutis cry?"

"Oh, yeah. Like a baby."

Lincoln could understand better why Yesutis seemed to hate Franklin. He asked, "Mom, can I have a glass of water?"

She got up and went to the kitchen. She was in a better mood than that morning, when they had almost gone for each other's throats. Roy got up and followed her. Lincoln heard them laughing and began to think that maybe he'd been wrong about Roy.

They returned to the living room, and Lincoln's mother handed him a glass of orange juice with ice. "This is better for you." She peeked under the washcloth on his knee and made a face. She asked Roy, "Do you think we should take him to the doctor?"

"No. Take him in tomorrow if it's still swollen." Roy sighed as he sank into their plush couch. "I tore up my knee on a Sunday, too. Playin' football at Golden Gate Park. It went out on a cheap-shot tackle by some beer-belly from Daly City. Can't use it too much. That's why I have this." He patted at his stomach, round as a kiddie-size basketball.

"I hope that don't happen to me. I mean, I hope my knee'll be OK."

"It looks bruised, maybe wrenched a little. You'll be all right." Then he added, "So, when do you play Franklin?"

"Tuesday," Lincoln responded.

"But you know, with your knee like this, Coach may not put you in."

Lincoln thought about it for a moment. Coach Yesutis would probably be upset. Or maybe not.

Lincoln went to soak himself in the tub. After dinner he watched television and then started on his homework. He had math to do and a geography report on Egypt, where the longest river in the world flowed and flowed.

Chapter 9

In the morning Lincoln's knee was still swollen and throbbing. In bed, he turned onto his hip, facing the wall. He was too scared to look at his knee. Finally, he raised himself to a sitting position, stretched and yawned, and parted the curtains to check out the day. The storm had come and gone, leaving behind a sky that was as cold and blue as the ocean.

"Lincoln," his mother called. She was in the kitchen, cooking. "It's after seven. *¡Ándale!*"

Lincoln pushed back the blankets and carefully rolled up the legs of his pajama bottoms. He was hoping that the knee wouldn't look as bad as it felt.

"Aw, man," he muttered. The knee was large and purple and hard as a nut. It was worse than he'd expected. He slowly maneuvered his legs out of bed and stood up shakily. He opened a drawer and pulled out a sweater, which he put on. Lincoln didn't like bathrobes. They reminded him of old people.

As he walked down the hall, he could hear the hiss and crackle of *papas*. He smelled green onions and his stomach knotted around his morning hunger. Last night's Chinese food, delicious as it was, hadn't done anything for him. The same with pizza—he could eat five slices, but he never felt satisfied. Just stuffed.

"Lincoln," his mother said, "pour yourself a glass of milk." She looked down at his knee, which he was favoring. "How is it? Does it still hurt?"

Lincoln answered yes as he limped to the refrigerator. The milk carton was nearly empty, so instead of getting a glass he chugged from the carton.

"*Ay, cochino,*" his mother said. She scraped the *huevos* and a pile of steaming *papas* onto a plate.

The newspaper was on the table. He pulled out the sports section and shook his head when he read, "Warriors Blown Away." The Warriors, as usual, had lost to the Lakers, and big—129–102.

Flaco whined on the front porch. Lincoln thought of letting him in, but he didn't feel like walking all the way through the living room to the front door. His knee was hurting. And anyway, breakfast was ready. He sat down, took up the bottle of ketchup, and laced his *papas*. He spooned *salsa* over the ketchup and started to eat.

His mother sat down with a refilled coffee cup. "If your leg is not better by tomorrow, you're going to the doctor."

"It'll be OK," Lincoln mumbled.

"*En serio. Vas a tener que ir.* You have to go."

Lincoln didn't like doctors. He would rather lie in bed with a fever, flu, blood poisoning, or broken bones than see a doctor. He didn't like injections. He would rather get smacked in the mouth in a behind-the-backstop fight than have some nurse approach him with a needle glistening with strange liquids.

Lincoln ran a tortilla across his plate, smearing the egg yolk. He looked up at his mother, wiped his mouth with a thumb, and said, "Can you write me a note?"

"A note?"

"I wanna stay home." He drank the last of the milk from the carton and added, "Just for the morning. I'll go to school in the afternoon."

He was thinking of basketball practice. He had to be there. It was the day before the game, and if he didn't show up, Coach would think he was afraid to play Franklin.

"Let me see the knee," his mother said.

Lincoln scooted back in his chair and, wincing, rolled up the leg of his pajamas.

"*Ay, Dios,*" she said, setting her coffee cup on the table. "You better stay home all day today."

"I can't, Mom. I have to go to practice."

"*No puedes correr con esa rodilla.* You can't run on that knee."

"I'm not planning to. I'll dress for practice, but I won't play." It was a lie. If Coach Yesutis told him to play, he would have no choice.

While his mother got ready for work, Lincoln hobbled into the hall and looked up Monica's number in the telephone book. There were six Torreses in the phone book, and he had to call three before he got the right one. He'd been scared of getting her mother, or worse, her father. But Monica answered the phone.

"Hi, Lincoln. How's the leg?" she asked. She didn't sound surprised to hear from him. "I'm really sorry that you hurt yourself."

"It's my knee, not my leg." Lincoln winced as he sat down on the couch. "I won't be there this morning."

"Are you going to go to the doctor?"

"No. I'm just gonna rest. But I'll be at school this afternoon. Can I see you at lunch?" In the background, he could hear the sound of a hair dryer—her mother getting ready for work.

"I'll be in the library. I didn't do my homework for English over the weekend." Monica paused. "Did you really eat venison?"

"Yeah. It was good. You don't believe me?"

"Not really. I also didn't believe you when you said where you went to church. There's no Saint Jay."

Lincoln bit his lip to keep from laughing. "Yeah, well, maybe I didn't go to church, but I did eat deer meat. Go ahead and ask James."

"That sounds gross. And cruel."

"That's what his parents were serving. I couldn't tell them, 'No, I don't eat deer meat. Please feed me bologna.'"

Monica laughed softly and said she would see him at school.

Lincoln hung up and chuckled to himself about getting caught lying. He had not been to church in nearly a year.

He returned to the kitchen, where his mother was searching for her keys. An aura of perfume hovered around her.

"Mom, you overdid the perfume." He fanned a hand in front of his face and pinched his nose.

"People like it," she said without looking up. Her mouth was made perfect by lipstick, and her hair, which had been mussed only a few minutes ago, was brushed into place. An expensive bracelet, a gift from Roy, jangled on her wrist. She smoothed her dress and picked a piece of lint off her sleeve.

"I'm goin' back to bed," Lincoln said. "Breakfast was real good. I'll do the dishes later."

"Rest your leg," his mother advised as she hurried down the hall to grab her briefcase and portfolio from the closet. "*Te llamo más tarde.* I'll call you later. *Adiós.*"

Lincoln returned to his bedroom, where he lay down with a sigh, being careful not to bump his knee. He heard the front door open and close, and a moment later heard a click-click on the kitchen floor.

It was Flaco, searching for his dog crunchies. Lincoln smiled and laughed for no reason at all. He was glad he had Flaco, even if he was a gift from a father he hadn't seen in years.

Flaco showed his face in Lincoln's doorway. His eyes were full of watery tenderness. He barked and wagged his tail. Lincoln got up, went to the kitchen, and fried Flaco an egg.

"Flaco, you're a little pig," Lincoln remarked playfully. He ruffled his fur as the dog ate in noisy chomps. He pressed on Flaco's hurt leg, and when the dog didn't whine, he decided to take off the bandage. The thing was filthy, useless. Flaco kept on eating as Lincoln snipped the bandage and unraveled it. The fur was damp and matted, but otherwise the leg looked healed.

"You're good as new." Lincoln grinned as he washed his hands at the kitchen sink. "No motorcycle can kill you."

Lincoln returned to his bedroom and rolled back into bed. He pushed in a cassette by Ice-T, but the music was too loud and upsetting with its rap about drugs on the street. It reminded him of Tony, whose favorite singer was also Ice-T. He wondered about Tony. He pictured his *carnal* kicking off to school, not carrying any books. He would be walking up Dolores, sidestepping drunks and homeless people. He would be passing the thrift shop, where he might stop to peek in the window; inside, the old man would be sitting in his recliner.

In the quiet of a Monday morning with no school, Lincoln fell asleep. The heat of two blankets made him sweat, and his sleep was hard and deep.

He woke when he heard the scraping of a chair. Footsteps sounded in the kitchen, and he thought he heard the rustle of newspaper. Groggily, he raised himself onto an elbow as Flaco jumped down and began to bark. Lincoln heard a voice and wondered why his mother was home. Maybe she's checking on me, he thought. He got out of bed slowly, straightening the collar of the sweater he was still wearing. He looked in his mirror and combed his hair with his fingers.

He hobbled down the hall into the kitchen and was startled to find a man looking at him, just looking, a screwdriver in his hand. The man's sweatshirt was splattered with paint, but his jeans were dark blue, new.

"Who are you?" Lincoln asked loudly. "Whatta ya doin'?"

The intruder turned away swiftly, sending a chair crashing to the floor, and hurried toward the front door, not running but not walking either. Lincoln, hobbling after him, threw his mother's Have-a-Nice-Day coffee cup and it shattered against the wall, just above the man's head. Lincoln wished that he had James's boomerang. He could bring that guy down like a squirrel. Crack open his thieving brains.

The intruder didn't look back. He was out the door and down the porch steps before Lincoln could stop him.

"Don't come back!" Lincoln screamed, fists curled tightly. "I'll mess with you, man." He picked up a sprinkler and threw it as far as he could. The sprinkler cartwheeled and kicked up grass. It was nothing like a boomerang. The intruder rounded Mr. Schulman's hedge unscathed.

Lincoln, chest heaving, stood on the steps with Flaco at his side. The intruder was gone. The neighborhood was once again peaceful. Two sparrows were feeding in the bushes, and leaves scuttled across the winter lawn.

It's sorry, Lincoln thought. What had sent them away from the Mission District had caught up with them in Sycamore—a break-in.

He returned inside to right the chair and try to piece the coffee cup together.

Chapter 10

Lincoln nailed shut the front door, which the intruder had pried open, his breath white in the cold air. Flaco lay on the steps, paws pressed together. He blinked every time the hammer banged against the wood.

"I don't believe this. . . . People are always trying to rip us off," Lincoln muttered as he stood back and examined the door. It looked broken. He went back in through the back door.

He called his mother's office and got her answering machine. "We're out of the office at the moment, but if you . . ." Lincoln hung up. He didn't feel like talking to a machine, even if it spoke in his mother's voice.

He wandered into the kitchen, opened the refrigerator, looked around, and closed it without tearing into the plate of leftover chicken. He wasn't hungry. His heart had slowed, but he still felt wired. He bent a teaspoon into a U and threw it in the sink. He wished he could have caught the guy. Then he thought, No, he probably had a gun or a knife.

Lincoln tried his mother's office one more time and then he dressed, stuffed his gym clothes into his backpack, and started off to school, limping. It was a quarter to twelve, and Monica would be waiting in the library. He pictured himself as Frankenstein, minus the stitches on the brow and the electrodes protruding from the neck. Lincoln had to laugh, but he winced when his foot came down awkwardly on a rock. He walked more carefully from then on.

He looked around, anxious because he thought the guy might come back. But probably not. Lincoln had scared him. He saw a guy in jeans and a 49ers jacket get into a blue '66 Nova. Could that be him? Lincoln's mind went wild. He memorized the car's license plate, and the car drove away, scattering leaves. But, Lincoln reasoned, no thief would stick around the scene of the crime, especially in Sycamore.

He stopped at the 7-Eleven for a pack of gum and a soda, which he drank standing near the trash can outside the store. A car pulled up and a guy got out. Lincoln wondered if it might be the thief. But the guy was wearing jeans with the knees ripped out, and the thief's jeans had been new. He looked at his watch: 11:55. Lincoln gulped the remainder of the soda and hurried off.

At school, he handed his mother's note to the secretary in the office.

The principal, Mr. Kimball, was hiking up his pants as he walked past Lincoln. "We're going to beat Franklin, right, Mr. Mendoza?"

"Yeah," Lincoln said without much energy. He didn't feel like talking basketball.

"Come on, where's the spirit?" the principal asked as he disappeared through the doorway. Now that it was lunch period, students were beginning to fill the hallway.

Lincoln thanked the secretary for his pink admittance slip and walked over to the library. Monica was at a table, biting into her apple furtively because no food was allowed in the library.

As he approached her, she looked up, her face pink and happy. She beat her pencil against the tabletop. "How's the knee? I'm really sorry that I tripped you."

"You didn't trip me. I scrubbed." He took a seat,

heaving his backpack into the empty chair next to him. He wanted to tell her about the break-in at his house, but he didn't know how. He looked up at the clock. Out of the corner of his eye, he could see the librarian at her desk, a sweater draped around her shoulders. He took off his sweater and said, "It's warm in here."

"Is anything wrong?" Monica asked, pushing her books away. She looked at him with concern. "Your knee isn't that bad, is it?"

"It's bad. But that's not the problem."

"What is it, then?"

Lincoln looked back at the clock. "I don't wanna talk 'bout it."

"Come on, Linc," she urged cheerfully. He noticed her blush was brighter on one cheek than the other.

"I *said* I don't want to talk about it," he snapped.

Monica's smile flattened into a line.

Lincoln tried to hold her hand, but she pulled it away. He felt lousy. His knee was busted, his house nearly ripped off, and Tony was no longer his *carnal*. And now Monica was mad. Lincoln got up, faked a smile, and, gathering his sweater and backpack, said, "I have homework to do. I'll see you later."

He turned around and walked out of the library. He knew it was stupid to get up and leave her. Now she would think he was a jerk. But he couldn't help himself. He returned to the administration building, where the secretary was eating popcorn and reading a magazine. It was her lunchtime. Lincoln hesitated to bother her.

"Mrs. Diggers, can I use the phone?" He wanted to try again to tell his mother about the break-in.

She turned some pages of her magazine and, without looking up, said, "No. You know the rule."

The rule was that you couldn't use the phone unless you had a broken leg, broken glasses, or generally were close to death. Last year one of the kids, feigning sickness, used the phone to order a pizza. The principal and the secretary had to help pay for the pizza when it arrived. That was the last straw.

Lincoln left without pestering her. He put down his backpack and put on his sweater. The sky was once again gray as slate. For the remainder of the lunch period, Lincoln sat on a cement bench sharpening a popsicle stick into a wooden knife and thinking of Tony and tomorrow's basketball game. He could picture Tony running up and down the court, and Coach Ramos clapping his hands and telling his players to play tough.

When the bell sounded, Lincoln went to geography, where he sat down to a multiple-choice quiz—thirty questions he thought were a cinch. He rolled his pencil between his palms, feeling smart. He had been reading about Egypt for longer than he could remember.

After geography he went to science and learned for the first time that the earth revolved around the sun. He had always thought it was the other way around.

He had a lot of questions regarding science. He wondered, for one, how rivers could run uphill. And why clouds could float when they were weighted down with gallons of water. But the questions were hard to ask.

The bell sent students out the doors to mingle and talk in the halls before the next class. Lincoln rose slowly. When he heaved his backpack onto his shoulder, his Air Jordans kicked him in the jaw. He slapped his backpack and hobbled to the door.

On his way to English, he saw Monica in the

hallway looking worried, biting a red fingernail. She called out, "Lincoln, I want to talk with you," but he ignored her and hurried off, a spark of pain in his knee. When he turned around to see if she was following him, she wasn't there.

English was his last class before practice. Lincoln walked slowly to the gym. He found Coach Yesutis shooting hoop by himself, his face already sweaty, his gray sweats sagging on his large, dumpy body. He shot from ten feet out and missed. Coach turned around when he heard footsteps. "Get dressed, Mendoza."

The janitor was running a dust mop across the gym floor, which gleamed and smelled of new polish. The overhead heater was blowing warm, dusty air.

"Coach, I gotta talk to you," Lincoln said, letting his backpack slide onto the floor. He remembered Roy's story about playing ball with Yesutis. For the first time, Lincoln realized the 1970 championship banner at Franklin was from the year Coach Yesutis had opened his mouth and Frankie Pineda had smacked him for running down Mexicans. It was the year Franklin won the Peninsula championship and Columbus was runner-up.

Coach Yesutis, dribbling the ball from his left hand to his right, moved in on a slow lay-up, one that a third grader could make. "What is it?"

"I hurt my knee. It's pretty bad."

Coach tucked the ball under his arm and commanded, "Get dressed. You don't have time to be hurt."

"It's serious." Lincoln rolled up his pant leg. "Check it out."

Coach didn't bother to look. Instead, he moved to another hoop when the janitor came to sweep the court he was on. Coach yelled, "Come on, don't be a crybaby. Get dressed, Mendoza."

Crybaby, Lincoln thought. I know more about you than you think.

James and Durkins came in with Grady. They were eating candy bars and licking flakes of potato chips from their fingers.

"Hey, Linc!" James shouted. Lincoln waved at them, forcing a smile. They all went into the locker room, where Lincoln sat on a bench, his head in his hands. He didn't know what to do. If he left, Coach would accuse him of not sucking it up in a tough moment. If he stayed, he could hurt his knee even worse. Lincoln punched the locker and turned the combination.

He got dressed and went out to the court, trying not to limp. He took a basketball from a canvas army bag and dribbled the ball, testing his knee. Under the overhead lights the knee looked more purple than ever.

Then Lincoln remembered his mother. He tossed the ball to Grady and went into Coach's office to use the telephone. He dialed quickly because he didn't want Coach to come in and yell at him for using the phone without asking.

On the fourth ring, he got his mother. "Mom, bad news. Our house was broken into."

"¡Qué!" she screamed. "Espérame un momento. Wait a minute." She put him on hold and then returned. "¿Nuestra casa? Our house?"

"Yeah, some guy broke open the door. I nailed it shut, so you have to use the back door."

"What were you doing? Were you in the house?"

Embarrassed, he told her he'd been asleep. Lincoln looked up at the clock. It was 3:42. "Mom, I gotta go."

"Where are you right now?"

"At school. At practice."

"I want you to meet me at home right away."

Lincoln looked down at Coach's desk. He saw the lineup for the Franklin game, and he was among the starters. He looked up and saw a photograph of Yesutis standing with Chris Mullins. Yesutis was grinning like a fool.

"I can't, Mom. I'm practicing."

"You better come," she said threateningly. "Did he hurt you?"

"No, I'm all right. But I threw your coffee cup at him and broke it."

"Did you get him?"

"No, I missed the *vato.*"

"Did you call the police?"

Lincoln hadn't thought to call the police. In his old neighborhood, you called the police only when someone was either run over or mugged. Or killed.

"No. I didn't call them. Mom, I'll be home as soon as I finish practice." He hung up without saying good-bye and returned to the gym, where he took shots and tried to run through the offenses without limping. But his knee was troubling him, and after twenty minutes of practice, he sat down without permission. Coach Yesutis stared at him angrily. Lincoln rubbed his swollen knee and ran a towel across his face while he watched his teammates run through drills.

When practice was over, Coach pointed at Lincoln and said, "Mendoza, you're not playing tomorrow. You don't know how to hang."

Lincoln looked up. "It's fine with me. Franklin's going to win. Like in '70."

"Whatta you talkin' 'bout?"

"You know. When you played."

"What do you mean?"

"*Hombre,* you know what I mean."

Coach wet his lips, studying Lincoln, who wouldn't look away. The gym went still. The heater clicked off and the breathing of sweaty players quieted. Muttering, the coach turned away, draped a towel over his shoulder, and went into his office.

The other players, with towels and basketballs in their arms, walked past Lincoln. They didn't know what to say to him. Lincoln remained slouched on the bench, a chill creeping up his back now that the sweat had dried.

He was the last to shower. When James asked if Lincoln wanted to walk home with him, Lincoln waved him off without looking at him. He wanted to be alone. He sat in the locker room, watching shadows creep across the cement floor. Then he limped home in the dark.

Chapter 11

By the time Lincoln arrived home, Roy was on the porch screwing new hinges into the front door. Flaco was watching him. Lincoln's mother, on her knees and bundled into a ski jacket, was holding a flashlight steady on Roy's work. She looked up, startled, and saw Lincoln. She let out her breath and said, "*Ay, ya llegaste.* You're home. Are you okay? Tell me what happened."

Lincoln climbed the steps, careful not to bend his knee, and took the flashlight from his mother. While he ran his free hand through Flaco's fur, which was damp from rolling on the lawn, he watched what Roy was doing.

"Well, I woke up and this dude was in the house. Flaco was barking. I was in bed and thought it was you, Mom."

"Me?"

"Yeah, I thought you had come home for something."

Lincoln helped steady the door as Roy, red-faced with effort, tightened a screw. Roy looked at Lincoln and Lincoln looked at Roy, their breath mingling in the cold night air. They both said "hi" and smiled.

They went inside to a dinner of *enchiladas, sopa,* and *frijoles.* Lincoln's mother had come home early after the telephone call and had had time to boil beans and bring down a steak from the freezer. Lincoln and Roy feasted like starved warriors.

Lincoln's mother was still worrying. She twisted

her napkin until it fell apart in shreds. "Do you think he'll come back?"

Neither Lincoln nor Roy looked up when they said "naw." They were busy scooping up the meat with rips of tortilla.

"Do you think he works this area?"

Again Roy and Lincoln grunted no.

Lincoln's mother said, "You took Flaco's bandage off. How's his leg?" Flaco lay near the butcher block, blinking sad eyes. Later he would get a handful of scraps and a send-off to the back porch.

"His leg is better."

Roy, running his napkin over his mouth, asked, "How's your knee?"

"It hurts. Coach Yesutis made me practice. But I stopped when it started hurting." Lincoln pushed away his plate. "He says I can't start."

Roy let his napkin drop onto his empty plate and nibbled on his last piece of tortilla. "What a punk. I'll be there tomorrow to straighten him out if he gives you trouble."

Lincoln liked that. He pictured Roy and his coach throwing punches in front of the entire school. He gathered the plates, but when he started to do the dishes, his mother shooed him away. "Go bathe. You need to soak your knee."

Lincoln felt relieved. He was tired. He ran the water scalding hot and nearly cried as he lowered his body into the bath piled high with bubbles. He soaked, scrubbed, and went limp with laziness. The water felt good.

After he got out, dried off, and dressed, he went into the living room, combing his hair. His mother said, "Oh, I forgot to tell you that you got some mail. It's on the mantel."

Lincoln picked up a small envelope with no return address. Tearing it open, he took out four dirty one-dollar bills. It was from Tony—the bet was paid. Lincoln looked up at his mother when she asked, "Who's the letter from?"

"It's not a letter. Just money. Remember the 49ers bet with Tony? He's paid up."

Roy, who was on the couch, rattled the newspaper and said, "Yeah, I remember the game. The 'Niners clobbered them."

His mother said she didn't remember. She asked if Lincoln wanted dessert, but he said no. He said good night, went to his bedroom, and did his Spanish homework, the easiest, and some of his English homework, the next easiest. But Tony kept coming back to his mind. Lincoln recalled the time when they were seven and went door to door looking for work with a broom and poor-boy grins. They figured they would be rich by lunchtime. But they were hired to sweep only one driveway, for which they were paid a dollar. They bought a soda and a bag of sunflower seeds and sat in the bleachers of a playground, watching older kids run around laughing and beating each other with plastic bats.

Lincoln closed his books and, sighing, switched off his lamp. He closed his eyes, and pictures of Tony flashed through his mind as he edged toward sleep.

The next morning his mother came to his bedroom. "*Déjame ver esa rodilla.* Let me see your knee."

Lincoln, rubbing his eyes, screamed, "*Ay!* Your hands are cold," when his mother reached under the blankets for his leg.

She rolled up the leg of his pajama bottoms and looked at his knee, her brow knitted with worry. "Does it hurt?"

Lincoln raised his leg and said, "Only when I do this." He crossed his eyes and let his tongue fall out.

"*¡En serio!*" his mother snapped.

"Naw, it's OK." He rose up on his elbows and parted the curtain. The day was overcast and cold, but the trees were still: no wind, no spiraling leaves, no squirrels jumping from limb to limb.

His mother left his bedroom, saying, "You'd better clean up your room. It's dirty. *¡Ándale!* I'll fix you breakfast."

Lincoln got up slowly. He hobbled to his dresser for a fresh T-shirt, socks, and jeans. He picked up a sweater from the floor, smelled the armpits, and decided it was not that bad.

Lincoln ate and went to school. He dreaded running into Monica, so he sneaked up and down the hallways between classes. He felt stupid. Why would he want to give her the brush-off? Between history and Spanish they nearly bumped into one another. Monica, who was laughing with a friend, suddenly stopped. She looked down and walked away, leaving Lincoln biting his lip.

He ate lunch on a cement bench. He could hear the pep band in the cafeteria and imagined the cheerleaders jumping about like the sparrows he watched on the dead lawn. He ripped into his sandwich—tuna today—and threw a crust at the sparrows, who scattered upward then came down to peck at his offering. He crunched on barbecue potato chips and wondered what his breath would be like. Tuna sandwich and barbecue potato chips—a deadly combination. He reached into his lunch bag and was glad to find an apple, even though it was bruised.

Durkins walked by with a hot dog in his hand. "Hey, bro," he said. "How come you ain't in the cafeteria? Coach is going to introduce the players."

Lincoln bit into his apple and said, "I don't like those things."

Durkins cleared his throat. "Sorry you're not startin'."

"It's better I don't. Anyway, I hate to say it, but I think you're gonna lose."

"Why do you say 'you,' not 'we'? Aren't you one of us?"

"It's not that."

"Then what's the big deal?"

"Nothin'."

"Nothin'? Why'd you say we're gonna lose?"

Lincoln got up, shaking out his lunch bag onto the lawn for the sparrows. Without looking at Durkins, he said, "I got homework to do. I'll see you at practice." That was when Coach Yesutis would gather his players around him for a pep talk and rap about school pride.

Lincoln wandered in the direction of the library. The students were leaving the cafeteria, the pep band still blowing hard on trumpets and trombones. The drums hurt Lincoln's ears, and someone bumped against his knee. He climbed the steps of the library to get out of the way. When he turned, he saw Monica at the table, alone. He looked back at the crowd. Coach Yesutis, in an ill-fitting suit and a Columbus hat with a plume, was marching among the students. Lincoln thought he looked like an idiot. He turned around, saw Monica again, and figured he should apologize to her. Sighing, head down, he walked in.

The librarian looked up, stern-faced. Lincoln forced a smile at her and walked over to the table where Monica sat. She glanced up and looked down quickly, her pencil moving more busily across the page.

"Hi," he said.

Monica turned a page in her binder.

"I'm sorry about yesterday. It's weird, but our house got broken into."

Monica stopped writing for a second, then started again, biting her lip.

"Yeah, I was home and this guy busted open the front door." Lincoln saw a half-eaten apple hidden between a pile of books and her backpack. He picked it up, tossed it into the air, bit into it, and said, "I just had a tuna sandwich and I need all the breath control I can get."

Monica swiped the apple from his hand. "Lincoln, you're selfish."

Lincoln thought about that for a moment. Maybe it was true. He swiped the apple back from her and took another bite. The librarian hurried over and said firmly, "No eating here."

"But I'm hungry," Lincoln pleaded.

"Eat outside," she said. "I can smell tuna sandwich on you."

Monica and Lincoln looked at one another, almost cracking up. Monica gathered her books and sweater and they left.

"Is it true about your house?"

"Yeah. But there's a lot of other things bothering me, too. Tony, *mi carnal,* is mad at me."

Monica stopped to put on her sweater.

"Why is he mad?"

"It's a long story. It has to do with a *viejo* at a thrift store in the city."

"Thrift store?"

"Yeah. As I said, it's a long story. I don't know

how I can explain it. It's one of those things where you had to be there to know what I'm saying. You know what I mean?"

"I think so," Monica answered, unsure.

They walked in silence, and when they came to a bench they sat down and watched two squirrels claw up a pine tree and disappear among the branches. Lincoln thought of taking her hand, but he knew better. He was glad when the bell sounded—the temptation was too great.

"I have algebra," Monica said, shouldering her backpack. She took two sticks of gum from her purse and gave one to Lincoln.

"I have geography," Lincoln said as he unwrapped the gum and pushed it into his mouth. "You're coming tonight, aren't you?"

"Of course."

Lincoln walked Monica to her classroom and then had to run, hurt leg or not, to his class. He couldn't risk getting a tardy slip.

After school he gathered his books and walked slowly to the gym, his untied laces swinging about his ankles. James caught up with him.

"Coach shouldn't have talked to you like that, Linc," James said, swinging a pair of Air Jordans and biting into a Baby Ruth. "He could see your knee is busted."

Lincoln, one hand in his pocket and the other gripping the strap of his backpack, just shook his head and said, "We're gonna get whipped."

"No, we're not. We beat 'em last time."

"That was last time, *loco*."

"We're a better team."

"That's what you think."

James didn't say anything. He followed Lincoln

into the gym, where most of the players were already in the bleachers. They were waiting for the pep talk. Grady, the center, was arguing with Zimmer, a guard, over a bag of Cornnuts. Buckley, the other guard and sometimes forward, was doing his math and counting on his fingers. The rest of them were pulling and pushing each other.

Coach was with the janitor, looking toward the ceiling and pointing to an overhead light that was out. He shook his head in agreement, laughed, and turned to his players. Clapping his hands, he shouted, "Listen up! Quiet! Grady, put those Cornnuts away. This is our last practice."

Immediately, the players stopped fooling around. Coach looked at his clipboard and, index finger working down the page, read out the starters—Grady, Zimmer, Buckley, Mitchell and Kaehler.

"Kaehler," James said. "I like my name. Snake James Kaehler—starter!"

Lincoln hurt inside. He had known that he wasn't going to start, but it still hurt.

James looked over at Lincoln and whispered, "Sorry, man. He's all wrong."

Coach Yesutis called out the backups to the center and point guard—Doyle and Parish. Then he sucked in a lot of old stinky gym air and began his lecture on manhood, tradition, and school spirit.

Lincoln tuned out by peeling a blister on his thumb.

Chapter 12

Lincoln came home from practice to find Flaco gnawing on a newspaper. A rubber band was caught between his teeth.

"Whatta ya doing?" Lincoln laughed. He went down to his good knee and worked the rubber band back and forth like dental floss until it came out. He shot the slobber-covered rubber band into the bushes and went inside.

It was a quarter after four, more than three hours before game time. To kill time, Lincoln did some of his homework, while Flaco paced from room to room. That's how I feel, Lincoln mused, even though I'm not playin'—nervous.

He took a hot bath and was getting out when he heard a noise in the kitchen—a rustle of newspaper and a bump against a chair. Lincoln's heart began to pound. He pulled a framed picture off the wall and, towel wrapped around his waist, tiptoed down the hallway. The thief's back, Lincoln thought. I'll slam this guy's face and make him pay.

But it was his mother putting groceries away. Lincoln said, "Hi, Mom," and she jumped, dropping a bundle of spinach, and held a hand over her heart.

"*Ay, Dios.*" She bent down to pick up the spinach. "You scared me."

"You mean *you* scared *me.*"

"What are you doing with that picture?"

Lincoln turned it around. It was of him and Flaco standing on a rock, acting goofy. It had been taken right after his father left. To keep their minds off the breakup, he and his mother, with the new dog, had gone on weekend trips out of the city. The picture had been taken on one of their excursions.

"I thought you were the guy who broke into our house. I was going to hit you with it."

His mother made a face. "Get dressed. *Vas a pescar un catarro.* You're going to catch a cold."

They ate an early dinner of leftover *chile verde.* Lincoln downed two glasses of milk and ate three tortillas. He wasn't going to play, so why not eat like a king? He told his mother about how unfair Coach Yesutis was.

"Oh, honey, he's just a coach. That's how they are." She got up and poured herself a cup of coffee. "He wants his team to win, and if you're hurt, then he has to get another player."

"Naw, Mom, it's more than that." Lincoln didn't know how to explain it. "He just doesn't like me. It's because I'm from—or was from—Franklin. You heard what Roy said about Yesutis mouthin' off 'bout Mexicans."

His mother sipped her coffee. "He was young then. He's a grown man now."

"There's somethin' weird about him."

"There's something weird about all of us," she countered and crossed her eyes. "Don't worry, I'll be there tonight." Lincoln laughed and crossed his own eyes.

Lincoln gathered the dishes and set them in the sink. He was sorry he couldn't make his mother understand. He left her sipping her coffee and turning the pages of her appointment book. He went to his bedroom to gather his stuff. He folded his Columbus basketball uniform and sweats into his game bag along with his shoes, three pairs of socks, jock, tape, Band-Aids, water bottle, knee pads, and a candy bar. But he took out the candy bar and ate it, thinking he wouldn't be needing it for energy later. After all, he thought, I'm not going to play.

His mother drove him to school. "*Regreso más tarde*. I'll be back later. I need to pick up something at the drugstore," she said as she dropped Lincoln off. She started to drive off but braked and rolled down her power window. She stuck her head out. "Roy'll be coming. Look for him." Lincoln watched the red taillights of her Maxima grow small as they disappeared up the street.

It was a little before seven, and game time was seven-thirty. The gym was warm and bright. The pep band was setting up, the tuba honking like a fat goose. The cheerleaders stood in a circle, clapping their white-gloved hands, and a few parents were sitting on the Columbus side. The Franklin side was empty, except for the janitor, who sat alone in the top row of the bleachers eating a sandwich.

Lincoln went into the locker room, where most of the players were already dressed. He could see that they were nervous and unsure. They were arguing and punching each other playfully.

"Hey, Linc," James called, pinned against the lockers by Grady, who was trying to fit a jock over James's head. Bukowski had Mitchell in a headlock.

The players looked up at Lincoln. Bukowski straightened up and remarked, "Durkins says you said that we're goin' to lose. Why did you say that?"

"I just said what I think." Lincoln unlaced his shoes and stepped out of his pants. He wished he hadn't said that, but Durkins had caught him in a sour mood.

"Yeah? Well, I don't like how you think," Bukowski said. "You think you're special."

"No, I don't."

"You and your hurt knee."

Lincoln stared at Bukowski. He had never liked him, and he liked him even less now. "If you wanna throw some, anytime, big mouth."

They stared at each other, fists clenched and chests puffed out. Lincoln wasn't sure if he could take Bukowski, who he'd heard bit when he fought. But he wasn't going to back down, either. Lincoln backed down only when there was a gang of three or four. One guy didn't mean much. At worst, he could get beat up—a jab to the jaw, a head butt under the chin, a swift kick in the groin. With a gang, there was no chance.

They stared at each other, chest to chest. Finally, Bukowski slammed his locker shut and walked away. A few of the players followed him.

Lincoln dressed while James sat with him.

"Don't worry, Linc," James finally said. "If Bukowski gives you trouble, I'll stand with you. I've known him since first grade. He's a jerk."

Lincoln and James left the locker room together. They passed Coach Yesutis. He was standing with Mr. Kimball, who was jingling coins in his pockets. The principal patted Lincoln and James on the shoulders and said, "Get 'em."

James beamed, and Lincoln forced a smile.

The gym was noisy. Spectators, mostly kids from Columbus, were stomping their feet in the bleachers. A drummer joined the tuba player. The sound echoed off the walls. The cheerleaders were jumping about, and a man in a Christopher Columbus hat was selling popcorn and soda.

Lincoln joined the others in lay-ups, moving swiftly from the top of the key. His blood warmed, and he swiped the ball and practiced jump shots. His knee pained him a little, but it wasn't bad. Laughing to himself, he thought that Mr. Bubble had done wonders for the ligaments in his knee.

Lincoln searched the Columbus side of the bleachers for his mother and Roy. He searched for Monica. They weren't there, so he turned to the Franklin side. He could see Coach Ramos with players huddled around him. He made out faces of the players he knew—Louie Estrada, Eddie "Big Foot" Negrete, Warren Higgins, Danny Salinas, and Tony. Tony was a second-stringer, not a starter, but he played a good game. He was strong and knew how to use an elbow to bruise a rib with one whack.

Coach Yesutis called his team together. Lincoln, trying his best to get involved, jogged over with his teammates and clasped hands with the players on either side of him—Bukowski and Durkins. Their hands were wet with sweat.

"Play man-to-man," Coach said. "Press. We beat 'em last time—let's get them again. Watch Big Foot. He hurt us last time." Coach looked up at the clock when the buzzer sounded. One of the refs blew his whistle and yelled, "Three minutes!" to both coaches.

Coach Yesutis nodded. He turned to his players, who closed in, arm in arm now, as they chanted, "One, two, three—break!"

They broke, and the five starters stripped off their sweats and gathered at center court, where they shook hands with the starters from Franklin. The pep band stopped playing for the tip-off. The spectators grew quiet, and Coach Yesutis ran a towel over his face.

The first ref tossed the ball up, and the game started with Franklin in possession. They moved left, then passed, and Estrada shot from ten feet—*swish*.

Columbus moved up the court but lost the ball on a turnover. Franklin scored again.

Lincoln didn't care to watch the game. He scanned the bleachers on the Franklin side and spotted Vicky. She looked good, as usual, and Lincoln's heart leaped like a fish under his Columbus sweats. But it sank when he saw the dude sitting next to her—close. He wondered if the dude was her new boyfriend. He looked up and saw that the score was 13–7, Franklin. He returned his gaze to Vicky and knew for sure that the dude was her new boyfriend: he was holding her hand, feeding his face popcorn with his free hand.

Lincoln groaned and stared at the floor. When he looked up again he saw that it was 19–11, Franklin. He saw Danny Salinas push Bukowski, a subtle foul that wasn't called by either ref, and he saw Bukowski shove back, sending Salinas to the ground. A foul was called, and Bukowski raised his hand, his second personal.

"He's so dumb," Lincoln muttered to himself. "He can't handle pressure. The *menso*."

Lincoln heard his name being called from the bleachers. He turned around and saw his mother. "*Mi'jo*, when are you going to play?" Roy was with her, his necktie loosened and his hand in a bag of popcorn.

"I told you, I'm not. I've been benched," he said.

Coach Yesutis looked over at Lincoln and then at his mother. He didn't say anything, and his face was worried and wet with sweat. His team was getting clobbered.

Lincoln scanned the bleachers. Where's Monica?

he wondered. Pretending to stretch, he stood up for a better look. He spotted her near the entrance, in one of the last rows of the bleachers, and waved, a bright toothy grin cutting across his face. She waved back. She was with her father, or someone who looked like he might be her father. The guy looked grim and serious, a Mexican version of Mr. Schulman, all business.

Franklin was up 23–16 at halftime. As the Columbus players jogged into the locker room, the pep band let loose with the tuba and trombone, and the popcorn and soda man bellowed, "Get it hot. Get it cold."

Coach Yesutis yelled at his players, stinking the air with cuss words. Lincoln figured this was their game, not his.

Since he wasn't going to play, he left the locker room and jogged quickly over to the Franklin bench. He shook hands with Mr. Ramos, who was happy to see him. Tony muttered, "Hey, Linc," under his breath. It's a start, Lincoln thought. Tony was still hurt, but he would get over it. Lincoln returned to his seat.

Coach Yesutis glared at him. "Don't talk to them. They're the other team."

Lincoln ignored him. He sat on the bench and gripped a gym towel. He was feeling good. He was glad that Franklin was up, glad that Monica was in the bleachers, glad that his mother and Roy were there. He was even glad for Vicky. Why shouldn't she have a new boyfriend? After all, wasn't he trying to hit on Monica?

The second half started with Franklin scoring— Tony sinking one from the top of the key. Lincoln clapped for him without thinking, and Coach stared angrily in his direction. Lincoln looked at the floor, holding back a smile, feeling giddy because he was now understanding that he was a Franklin boy beneath a Columbus uniform. He was brown, not white; poor, not rich; city, not suburbia. He couldn't help where he lived now. As he sat on the sidelines he realized he couldn't deny who he was.

He watched the game, kneading his hurt knee, and in the last quarter when Coach Yesutis said, "Mendoza, you're goin' in," Lincoln shrugged his shoulders and said, "Why not?" He would break a sweat, make a few baskets, tease Big Foot, talk Tony back into friendship, shower, and after the game chug a Slurpee with James. He wasn't going to try to beat Franklin, but he wasn't going to let Columbus look like losers, either. Lincoln was going to play for himself, not school pride.

Lincoln got the ball and dribbled slowly up court, passed to James, who feigned left but cut right and passed back. Lincoln laid it in and raised a clenched fist when fans on the Columbus side of the bleachers stomped their feet. Lincoln's mom and Roy stood up, cheering.

A Franklin sub for Danny Salinas moved up the court, dribbling poorly. Lincoln slapped the ball from him and dribbled in for an easy lay-up.

Lincoln was getting into the groove of the game, hurt knee or not. He played tight against Louie Estrada, who was tired because he'd played most of the game, and blocked Estrada's shot fifteen feet out from the corner. Lincoln passed to James, who passed to Durkins, who took a shot and missed from the top of the key. But Lincoln pulled the ball down, chambered, and shot—*swish*.

Lincoln broke down the court, Tony running at his

side. Lincoln asked, "You mad?" Tony didn't answer him, but Lincoln thought he didn't look mad.

Franklin scored and was ahead 47–39 with three minutes left. Lincoln realized Columbus couldn't catch up. But he didn't care. He wanted the game to end. Coach Yesutis was getting out of hand, insulting his players and yelling at the refs for not calling fouls. He threw down his clipboard, and the spectators on the Franklin side booed him. Mr. Kimball tried to calm him down, and the tuba player covered Coach Yesutis's ranting by blowing hard enough to pop an eardrum.

Lincoln turned on the juice and scored three quick buckets. The Columbus side went wild, spilling popcorn and stomping paper cups. Lincoln pulled down a rebound and pushed up the court, sweat running from his face as he maneuvered between players and came to the boards untouched.

The game ended 52–46 with Lincoln heaving the ball from center court and missing the backboard altogether. Lincoln had narrowed the gap, but it was still a league loss. Exhausted, pinching his side, he turned to shake hands with the Franklin players— Louie Estrada and Eddie Big Foot—and Coach Ramos, who patted Lincoln on his back and said, "You scared us."

Lincoln smiled and jogged over to Tony, who was walking away. "I'm sorry. I was wrong."

"Later," Tony said, toweling his face. "You played a good game, as usual."

Smiling, Lincoln returned to the bench and stepped into his sweats. He shook hands with James, and even Bukowski, who said, "Good playin'."

Mr. Kimball asked Coach Yesutis why he hadn't put Lincoln in earlier. "I'm the coach," Yesutis yelled.

"He's got a bad attitude." Lincoln ignored him. He was too happy to bother with accusations.

"Coach—for now," the principal remarked as he walked away.

Coach Yesutis glared at Lincoln, who was waving at his mom and Roy. He snapped, "Mendoza, I wanna talk to you!" Stepping over the bench and between the players, he grabbed Lincoln roughly by the arm. Lincoln pushed him away and when Coach tried to grab him again, Roy stepped down and hollered, "Yesutis, Frankie Pineda is still looking for you."

Coach Yesutis turned to Roy. "Do I know you?"

"Franklin, 1970. You were second-string. Don't you remember?" Roy smiled as he stepped between the coach and Lincoln. "Don't mess with the boy."

"*Órale,*" Lincoln said under his breath. He would have liked to see Roy and Coach have it out in front of the entire school. But Coach walked away. Roy returned to Lincoln's mom. They told Lincoln to hurry up and shower so they could take him out to eat.

Lincoln waved to Monica, who waved back, then he hobbled into the locker room, where he showered and pampered his knee by lathering it with shampoo borrowed from Snake James.

Chapter 13

Lincoln woke up as the first light of dawn cut across his bedroom wall. He fixed himself a bowl of cereal and read the newspaper: the Warriors had beaten the Sacramento Kings, the lousiest team in the NBA. Still, it was a victory, Lincoln thought as he munched a mouthful of Cocoa Puffs.

He looked at the clock: 7:20. In fifteen minutes he would call Tony. In twenty minutes he would call Monica. He felt good. Last night he had scored six buckets and won back his friend Tony and, maybe, just maybe, won himself a new girlfriend.

Outside, Lincoln saw a hummingbird dip and hover at the feeder. He watched it drink and dart away as quickly as it had come. He returned his attention to the newspaper. The Warriors were still behind, but there was hope. The season wasn't even half over yet.

Flaco whined at the front door. Lincoln got up and peeked out the front window. Flaco was holding his army blanket between his teeth. Lincoln laughed, opened the door, and let Flaco in, minus the blanket.

"*¿Tienes hambre?* Are you hungry?" Lincoln asked as he fixed Flaco a bowl of Cocoa Puffs. Flaco lapped up the cereal, splashing milk on the floor.

Lincoln heard his mother stir in her bedroom, so he quickly gathered up Flaco's bowl. She didn't like the dog to eat cereal, especially not out of her bowls.

She came into the kitchen, tightening the belt to her robe. Her mussed hair was pushed to one side and her eyes were puffy from sleep.

"The hot water is hot," Lincoln said.

"The hot water is hot?" his mother mimicked playfully. "What kind of logic is that?" She opened the cupboard and took out the coffee beans and her grinder. "Are you hungry?"

"Naw, I had some cereal." Then he added, "I'm still full from the pizza." Lincoln, his mother, and Roy had gone out with the players from Franklin. After the altercation with Coach Yesutis, Lincoln had jogged over to talk to Coach Ramos, who asked him to join the Franklin team for pizza. Lincoln was happy. He shouted for his mother and Roy to come over, and Coach Ramos asked them to come along, too.

Lincoln was proud when Roy said they could order three large pizzas with the works and he would pick up the tab. He was even prouder when Roy talked about his own years playing for Franklin. Coach Yesutis's name came up once, and once was enough— Roy told the story of Frankie Pineda punching out Yesutis in a championship game in 1970. Everyone at the table cheered and laughed.

Big Foot asked Lincoln if he liked his new school, and Lincoln said, "It's all right." Danny Salinas asked if he had got into any fights. Lincoln said life at Columbus was a piece of cake, unlike at Franklin, where it was knuckle city every day.

Tony was quiet at first. He sipped his soda and chewed slowly on the same slice of pizza while others were working on their third and fourth slices. But after a while he joined the talk and began to look more and more in Lincoln's direction. Toward the end of the evening Tony told Lincoln that he had gone back to the thrift shop and bought the TV.

"It was only fifteen bucks," Tony said. "It even still works. It's gonna be your Christmas present, Linc."

That was last night. Now it was a new day in the same jeans and T-shirt, and the feeling was good. Lincoln looked at the clock: 7:40. Time to call Tony. He had a debt to pay—a four-dollar bet with Tony that the Kings would beat the Warriors. But it was the other way around, and when he'd paid this debt it would be even between them. On the third ring, he got Tony who whispered sleepily, "It's early, *hombre*."

"The Warriors won."

"¡*Órale!*" Tony yelled, his bedsprings squeaking. "I'll pick it up on Saturday. Be home, *ese*. We'll get in a game of one-on-one."

"I'll be here," Lincoln said as he hung up, smiling. He sucked in a roomful of breath, let it out, and sighed. "Now Monica."

Lincoln, heart thumping, punched in her phone number. Just as he began to stutter, "Hello," his mother started the hair dryer. It was better that way. He had things to say to Monica no one else should hear.

Glossary of Spanish Words and Phrases

abrazo	hug
aliviánate	lighten up
a lo mejor	maybe
¡ándale, muchacho!	hurry, kid!
¡apúrate!	hurry up!
¡ay Dios, que gente!	my God, what people!
bueno	good
buenos días	hello, good day
cansada	tired
carnal	brother, bro
carne asada	grilled meat
chale	I don't want to, no way
chamaco	kid
chavalo	kid, boy
chile verde	green chili stew
claro	of course
cochino	pig
con permiso	excuse me
con safos	a taunt, as in "What are you gonna do about it?"
de veras	really
en	in
en serio	seriously

escúchame	listen to me
Es medio tonto	He's sort of foolish
espérate	wait
ese	dude, guy
esto	this
frijoles	beans
gavacho	white person
gente	people
gordo	fat guy
hace mucho frio	I'm very cold
hacia calor	it was hot
hermano	brother
hijo	son
hombre	man
hombrecito	little man
huevos	eggs
limonada	lemonade
Llámalo	Call him
loca, loco	crazy
menso	fool
mi familia	my family
mi hermano	my brother
mi'jo	my son (affectionate)
muchacho	boy

muchachote	big boy
ni modo	no way, too bad
no sé	I don't know
¡órale!	come on!
papas	potatoes
perrito	little dog
¿por qué?	why
pronto	quickly
pues no	well, no
¡Qué grande te has puesto!	How tall you've become!
que loca	how crazy
¿Qué quieres?	What do you want?
queso	cheese
raza	Latino people
rodilla	knee
salsa	hot sauce
señor, señora	sir, ma'am
sí	yes
sopa	a rice dish
¿Tienes hambre?	Are you hungry?
tonto	stupid, fool
vato loco	crazy dude
vatos	guys

ven acá	come here
vendido	sellout
verdad	truth
vieja	old woman
viejo	old man
y esto	and this

Related Readings

CONTENTS

Endless Search

by Alonzo Lopez

*Like Lincoln Mendoza, you may have often
heard the question "Who do you think
you are?" As you read this poem, think
about how the speaker might respond to
such a question.*

Searching,
    forever searching.
Looking,
    but never finding.
Day and night,
    my eyes roam the world.
Searching,
    not knowing how to end
5 This search for myself.

from **Barrio Boy**

by Ernesto Galarza

What experiences do you recall from your first years in school? Like Lincoln, maybe you, too, have warm memories of your early schooling. In this excerpt from his memoir, Ernesto Galarza recounts his experiences entering school as a native speaker of Spanish.

We found the Americans as strange in their customs as they probably found us. Immediately we discovered that there were no *mercados* and that when shopping, you did not put groceries in a *chiquihuite.* Instead, everything was in cans or in cardboard boxes, or each item was put into a brown paper bag. There were neighborhood grocery stores at the corners and some big ones uptown, but no *mercado.* The grocers did not give children a *pilón;* they did not stand at the door and coax you to come in and buy, as they did in Mazatlán. The fruits and vegetables were displayed on counters instead of being piled up on the floor. The stores smelled of fly spray and oiled floors, not of fresh pineapple and limes.

Neither was there a plaza, only parks that had no bandstands, no concerts every Thursday, no Judases exploding on Holy Week, and no promenades of boys going one way and girls the other. There were no parks in the *barrio;* and the ones uptown were cold and rainy in winter, and in summer there was no place to sit except on the grass. When there were celebrations, nobody set off rockets in the parks, much less on the street in front of your house to announce to the neighborhood that a wedding or a baptism was taking place. Sacramento did not have a *mercado* and a plaza with the cathedral to one side and the *Palacio de Gobierno* on another to make it obvious that there and nowhere else was the center of town.

It was just as puzzling that the Americans did not live in *vecindades,* like our block on Leandro Valle. Even in the alleys, where people knew one another better, the houses were fenced apart, without central courts to wash clothes, talk, and play with the other children. Like the city, the Sacramento *barrio* did not have a place which was the middle of things for everyone.

In more personal ways we had to get used to the Americans. They did not listen if you did not speak loudly, as they always did. In the Mexican style, people would know that you were enjoying their jokes tremendously if you merely smiled and shook a little, as if you were trying to swallow your mirth. In the American style there was little difference between a laugh and a roar, and until you got used to them, you could hardly tell whether the boisterous Americans were roaring mad or roaring happy. . . .

America was all around us, in and out of the *barrio.* Abruptly we had to forget the ways of shopping in a *mercado* and learn those of shopping in a corner grocery or in a department store. The Americans paid no attention to the Sixteenth of September, but they made a great commotion about the Fourth of July. In Mazatlán, Don Salvador had told us, saluting and marching as he talked to our class, that the *Cinco de Mayo* was the most glorious date in human history. The Americans had not even heard about it.

In Tucson, when I had asked my mother again if

the Americans were having a revolution, the answer was, "No, but they have good schools, and you are going to one of them." We were by now settled at 418 L Street, and the time had come for me to exchange a revolution for an American education.

The two of us walked south on Fifth Street one morning to the corner of Q Street and turned right. Half of the block was occupied by the Lincoln School. It was a three-story wooden building, with two wings that gave it the shape of a double-T connected by a central hall. It was a new building, painted yellow, with a shingled roof that was not like the red tile of the school in Mazatlán. I noticed other differences, none of them very reassuring.

We walked up the wide staircase hand in hand and through the door, which closed by itself. A mechanical contraption screwed to the top shut it behind us quietly.

Up to this point the adventure of enrolling me in the school had been carefully rehearsed. Mrs. Dodson had told us how to find it, and we had circled it several times on our walks. Friends in the *barrio* explained that the director was called a principal, and that it was a lady and not a man. They assured us that there was always a person at the school who could speak Spanish.

Exactly as we had been told, there was a sign on the door in both Spanish and English, "Principal." We crossed the hall and entered the office of Miss Nettie Hopley.

Miss Hopley was at a roll-top desk to one side, sitting in a swivel chair that moved on wheels. There was a sofa against the opposite wall, flanked by two windows and a door that opened on a small balcony. Chairs were set around a table, and framed pictures hung on the walls of a man with long white hair and another with a sad face and a black beard.

The principal half-turned in the swivel chair to look at us over the pinch glasses that crossed the ridge of her nose. To do this she had to duck her head slightly as if she were about to step through a low doorway.

What Miss Hopley said to us we did not know, but we saw in her eyes a warm welcome, and when she took off her glasses and straightened up, she smiled wholeheartedly, like Mrs. Dodson. We were, of course, saying nothing, only catching the friendliness of her voice and the sparkle in her eyes while she said words we did not understand. She signaled us to the table. Almost tiptoeing across the office, I maneuvered myself to keep my mother between me and the *gringo* lady. In a matter of seconds I had to decide whether she was a possible friend or a menace. We sat down.

Then Miss Hopley did a formidable thing. She stood up. Had she been standing when we entered, she would have seemed tall. But rising from her chair, she soared. And what she carried up and up with her was a buxom superstructure, firm shoulders, a straight sharp nose, full cheeks slightly molded by a curved line along the nostrils, thin lips that moved like steel springs and a high forehead topped by hair gathered in a bun. Miss Hopley was not a giant in body, but when she mobilized it to a standing position, she seemed a match for giants. I decided I liked her.

She strode to a door in the far corner of the office, opened it, and called a name. A boy of about ten years appeared in the doorway. He sat down at one end of the table. He was brown like us, a plump kid with shiny black hair combed straight back, neat, cool, and faintly obnoxious.

Miss Hopley joined us with a large book and some papers in her hand. She, too, sat down and the questions and answers began by way of our interpreter. My name was Ernesto. My mother's name was Henriqueta. My birth certificate was in San Blas. Here was my last report card from the *Escuela Municipal Numero 3 para Varones* of Mazatlán, and so forth. Miss Hopley put things down in the book, and my mother signed a card.

As long as the questions continued, Doña Henriqueta could stay and I was secure. Now that they were over, Miss Hopley saw her to the door, dismissed our interpreter, and without further ado took me by the hand and strode down the hall to Miss Ryan's first grade.

Miss Ryan took me to a seat at the front of the room, into which I shrank—the better to survey her. She was—to skinny, somewhat runty me—of a withering height when she patrolled the class. And when I least expected it, there she was, crouching by my desk, her blond radiant face level with mine, her voice patiently maneuvering me over the awful idiocies of the English language.

During the next few weeks Miss Ryan overcame my fears of tall, energetic teachers as she bent over my desk to help me with a word in the preprimer. Step by step, she loosened me and my classmates from the safe anchorage of the desks for recitations at the blackboard and consultations at her desk. Frequently she burst into happy announcements to the whole class. "Ito can read a sentence," and small Japanese Ito, squint-eyed and shy, slowly read aloud while the class listened in wonder: "Come, Skipper come. Come and run." The Korean, Portuguese, Italian, and Polish first graders had similar moments of glory no less shining than mine the day I conquered *butterfly,* which I had been persistently pronouncing in standard Spanish as *boo-ter-flee.* "Children," Miss Ryan called for attention. "Ernesto has learned how to pronounce *butterfly!*" And I proved it with a perfect imitation of Miss Ryan. From that celebrated success, I was soon able to match Ito's progress as a sentence reader with "Come, butterfly, come fly with me."

Like Ito and several other first graders who did not know English, I received private lessons from Miss Ryan in the closet, a narrow hall off the classroom with a door at each end. Next to one of these doors Miss Ryan placed a large chair for herself and a small one for me. Keeping an eye on the class through the open door, she read with me about sheep in the meadow and a frightened chicken going to see the king, coaching me out of my phonetic ruts in words like *pasture, bow-wow-wow, hay,* and *pretty,* which to my Mexican ear and eye had so many unnecessary sounds and letters. She made me watch her lips and then close my eyes as she repeated words I found hard to read. When we came to know each other better, I tried interrupting to tell Miss Ryan how we said it in Spanish. It didn't work. She only said "oh" and went on with *pasture, bow-wow-wow,* and *pretty.* It was as if in that closet we were both discovering together the secrets of the English language and grieving together over the tragedies of Bo-Peep. The main reason I was graduated with honors from the first grade was that I had fallen in love with Miss Ryan. Her radiant, no-nonsense character made us either afraid not to love her or love her so we would not be afraid; I am not sure which. It was not only that we sensed she was with it, but also that she was with us.

Like the first grade, the rest of the Lincoln School was a sampling of the lower part of town where many races made their home. My pals in the second grade were Kazushi, whose parents spoke only Japanese; Matti, a skinny Italian boy; and Manuel, a fat Portuguese who would never get into a fight but wrestled you to the ground and just sat on you. Our assortment of nationalities included Koreans, Yugoslavs, Poles, Irish, and home-grown Americans.

Miss Hopley and her teachers never let us forget why we were at Lincoln: for those who were alien, to become good Americans; for those who were so born, to accept the rest of us. Off the school grounds we traded the same insults we heard from our elders. On the playground we were sure to be marched up to the principal's office for calling someone a wop, a chink, a dago, or a greaser. The school was not so much a melting pot as a griddle, where Miss Hopley and her helpers warmed knowledge into us and roasted racial hatreds out of us.

At Lincoln, making us into Americans did not mean scrubbing away what made us originally foreign. The teachers called us as our parents did or as close as they could pronounce our names in Spanish or Japanese. No one was ever scolded or punished for speaking in his native tongue on the playground. Matti told the class about his mother's down quilt, which she had made in Italy with the fine feathers of a thousand geese. Encarnación acted out how boys learned to fish in the Philippines. I astounded the third grade with the story of my travels on a stagecoach, which nobody else in the class had seen except in the museum at Sutter's Fort. After a visit to the Crocker Art Gallery and its collection of heroic paintings of the golden age of California, someone showed a silk scroll with a Chinese painting. Miss Hopley herself had a way of expressing wonder over these matters before a class, her eyes wide open until they popped slightly. It was easy for me to feel that becoming a proud American, as she said we should, did not mean feeling ashamed of being a Mexican.

The Americanization of Mexican me was no smooth matter. I had to fight one lout who made fun of my travels on the *diligencia* and my barbaric translation of the word into "diligence." He doubled up with laughter over the word until I straightened him out with a kick. In class I made points explaining that in Mexico roosters said "qui-qui-ri-qui" and not "cock-a-doodle-doo," but after school I had to put up with the taunts of a big Yugoslav who said Mexican roosters were crazy.

But it was Homer who gave me the most lasting lesson for a future American.

Homer was a chunky Irishman who dressed as if every day was Sunday. He slicked his hair between a crew cut and a pompadour. And Homer was smart, as he clearly showed when he and I ran for president of the third grade.

Everyone understood that this was to be a demonstration of how the American people vote for President. In an election, the teacher explained, the candidates could be generous and vote for each other. We cast our ballots in a shoe box and Homer won by two votes. I polled my supporters and I came to the conclusion that I had voted for Homer and so had he. After class he didn't deny it, reminding me of what the teacher had said—we could vote for each other but didn't have to.

The lower part of town was a collage of nationalities in the middle of which Miss Nettie Hopley kept school with discipline and compassion. She called assemblies in the upper hall to introduce celebrities like the police sergeant or the fire chief, to lay down the law of the school, to present awards to our athletic champions, and to make important announcements. One of these was that I had been proposed by my school and accepted as a member of the newly formed Sacramento Boys' Band. "Now, isn't that a wonderful thing?" Miss Hopley asked the assembled school, all eyes on me. And everyone answered in a chorus, including myself, "Yes, Miss Hopley."

It was not only the parents who were summoned to her office and boys and girls who served sentences there who knew that Nettie Hopley meant business. The entire school witnessed her sizzling Americanism in its awful majesty one morning at flag salute.

All the grades, as usual, were lined up in the courtyard between the wings of the building, ready to march to classes after the opening bell. Miss Shand was on the balcony of the second floor of Miss Hopley's office, conducting us in our lusty singing of "My Country tiz-a-thee." Our principal, as always, stood there like us, at attention, her right hand over her heart, joining in the song.

Halfway through the second stanza she stepped forward, held up her arm in a sign of command, and called loud and clear, "Stop the singing." Miss Shand looked flabbergasted. We were frozen with shock.

Miss Hopley was now standing at the rail of the balcony, her eyes sparkling, her voice low and resonant, the words coming down to us distinctly and loaded with indignation.

"There are two gentlemen walking on the school grounds with their hats on while we are singing," she said, sweeping our ranks with her eyes. "We will remain silent until the gentlemen come to attention and remove their hats." A minute of awful silence ended when Miss Hopley, her gaze fixed on something behind us, signaled Miss Shand, and we began once more the familiar hymn. That afternoon, when school was out, the word spread. The two gentlemen were the Superintendent of Schools and an important guest on an inspection.

I came back to the Lincoln School after every summer, moving up through the grades with Miss Campbell, Miss Beakey, Mrs. Wood, Miss Applegate, and Miss Delahunty. I sat in the classroom adjoining the principal's office and had my turn answering her telephone when she was about the building repeating the message to the teacher, who made a note of it. Miss Campbell read to us during the last period of the week about King Arthur, Columbus, Buffalo Bill, and Daniel Boone, who came to life in the reverie of the class through the magic of her voice. And it was Miss Campbell who introduced me to the public library on Eye Street, where I became a regular customer.

All of Lincoln School mourned together when Eddie, the blond boy everybody liked, was killed by a freight train as he crawled across the tracks going home one day. We assembled to say goodbye to Miss Applegate, who was off to Alaska to be married. Now it was my turn to be excused from class to interpret for a parent enrolling a new student fresh from Mexico. Graduates from Lincoln came back now and then to tell us about high school. A naturalist entertained us in assembly, imitating the calls of the meadowlark, the water ouzel, the oriole, and the killdeer. I decided to become a bird man after I left Lincoln.

In the years we lived in the lower part of town, La Leen-Con, as my family called it, became a benchmark in our lives, like the purple light of the Lyric Theater and the golden dome of the *Palacio de Gobierno* gleaming above Capitol Park.

In the Inner City

by Lucille Clifton

According to a popular saying, "Home is where the heart is." As you read this poem, think about where the speaker's heart is. What connections do you see between the speaker and Lincoln?

in the inner city
or
like we call it
home
5   we think a lot about uptown
and the silent nights
and the houses straight as
dead men
and the pastel lights
10 and we hang on to our no place
happy to be alive
and in the inner city
or
like we call it
15 home

I Yearn

by Ricardo Sanchez

*To Lincoln, the urban barrio has a special
quality. In this poem the speaker describes
what that special quality is.*

i yearn this morning
what i've yearned
since i left

     almost a year ago . . .

5 it is hollow
this
being away
from everyday life
in the barrios
10 of my homeland . . .
all those cities
like el paso, los angeles,
albuquerque,
denver, san antonio
     (off into chicano infinitum!);

15 i yearn
to hear spanish
spoken in caló—
that special way
chicanos roll their tongues
20 to form
words
which dart or glide;

i yearn
for foods
25 that have character
and strength—the kind
that assail yet caress
you with the zest of life;

more than anything,
30 i yearn, my people,
for the warmth of you
greeting me with "¿qué tal,
hermano?"
and the knowing that you mean it
35 when you tell me that you love
the fact that we exist . . .

Granny Ed and the Lewisville Raiders

by Rae Rainey

If you have ever been on a sports team, chances are that you, like Lincoln, have definite ideas about how coaches should treat their players. This short story is about a coach with a style all her own.

It never occurred to me that Granny Ed was different from other grandmothers. Her name was out of the ordinary, but she always said, "If your parents put a handle like Edwinalou on you, you'd prefer a nickname too." It made good sense to me. She had normal grandmother interests like knitting, baking, and attending my basketball games.

Basketball! I eat and sleep the sport, but right then I wished I'd never heard of it. Our high school team had basketball Trouble, and I mean Trouble with a capital *T*.

Coach Marshall was a super coach, and we had high hopes of finishing first in the district this year. What happened? December second, Coach Marshall had a car accident over by Murphy Junction. He ended up in the hospital with a broken back and will be in the hospital two months—plus a long convalescence. To make matters worse, the only other man teacher in our high school is Mr. LaFrance, who doesn't know whether you bounce, kick, or bury a basketball. That leaves the Lewisville Raiders coachless.

The team had gathered at our house, as usual, due to Granny Ed's weakness for feeding hungry ballplayers.

"Men, we've got troubles if the principal can't come up with someone to take Coach Marshall's place," Al James said, between huge bites of pizza.

"Wish my dad could help out, but he's working swing shift at the sawmill," said Leftie.

"If Grandpa Thor were still living, he would take over," I added sadly. "He was a great college coach before he died." The team nodded in sympathetic agreement and respect.

"If we could just get someone to come to the gym and supervise our practices, maybe we could stumble along until a replacement for Coach Marshall is found," Al said.

"That's easier said than done. All the teachers are already doubling up on classes," I said, feeling more discouraged every minute.

"Well, gentlemen, if a *body* is all you need at practice, I can certainly provide that," Granny Ed spoke from the doorway. "You're sure not going to let a little problem like this throw a monkey wrench in the Lewisville Raider team, are you?"

There was a long silence. I wanted to sink through the floor. Granny Ed at practice! Oh no! *You've really done it this time, Granny Ed*, I thought.

Al, who has a reputation for having a pretty cool head, was the first to speak. "You know, Granny Ed, I think if the principal OK's your offer, it would really help us out of a tough spot. We need help right now!"

The rest of the team nodded in approval.

That's how it all started. Granny Ed arrived promptly at three-thirty the next afternoon. Her knitting bag was under one arm, a newspaper under the other, and she was sporting the brightest pair of red tennis shoes I'd ever laid eyes on.

"Go right ahead with your practice, gentlemen. I'll just sit here and watch," she said, whipping out her spare knitting needle that was always secured in the thick braids on top of her head.

"OK, men, let's work on some man-to-man defense," Al yelled. "We've been pretty sloppy."

Buzzie and Leftie brought the ball down court. Mark Elingson was guarding Leftie, but with one quick move Leftie faked out Mark and went in for an easy shot.

"Run the play again," Al called out, "and this time, stay with your man, Mark."

Buzzie tossed the ball to Leftie. A quick move to his left and Leftie had another easy shot.

"What do you do with a left-handed shooter, Mark?" a voice shouted from the sidelines. Granny Ed leaped to her feet and was out on the floor, showing Mark exactly what he was doing wrong.

"You're positioning your body wrong for a left-handed shooter," she said. "And you, Al, you've been standing in the key at least ten seconds. Move in and out of there. In a game the referee would give the ball out-of-bounds to the other team," she scolded.

Al's face turned tomato-red, but he nodded in agreement. "Guess you're right, Granny Ed, but how do you know about basketball rules?"

"Gentlemen, I didn't sit for twenty-five years keeping statistics and watching Big Thor coach for nothing. There very little I don't know about basketball."

From then on, it was Granny Ed all the way. She worked us so hard and long our tongues were hanging out, but we all knew it was the best practice session we'd had all season.

"See you tomorrow, Granny Ed," the team yelled as we headed out the gym doors for home.

"Goodbye, gentlemen." Granny Ed waved back happily.

She hummed to herself as we headed toward home. Suddenly she stopped. "I didn't embarrass you, did I, Sprout?" she asked anxiously. "Did I come on a little too strong at practice?" She studied my face carefully.

"No, Granny, you did just fine," I said, trying to sound convincing. "You really helped us out." What could it hurt? It would only be for a few days.

They say bad luck runs in streaks, but for our Lewisville Raiders it ran as wide as the Colorado River. At the end of the week, there was no new basketball coach.

"It is a financial impossibility for our small district to pay the salary of another teacher-coach, boys. Until the school board finds a volunteer to take over, you will simply have to make do," Mr. Fisch told us. "It is something over which I have no control," he said, shuffling the papers on his desk nervously.

That day, after practice, we gathered in the gym to discuss our problem.

"Granny Ed, what are we going to do?" Al asked.

"Tomorrow night, gentlemen, you have your first league game against Darby. They're the defending champions in the league, but I believe you have the ability to beat them. You've worked long and hard in practice, and you're ready for any team. If you're willing to put up with an old lady for one game, I'll do my very best to help. What do you say, gentlemen?"

The startled players looked from one to another. I stared a hole through the gym floor. I just couldn't bear to watch what was going to happen. Whispers passed from player to player, and then Al stood up.

"Granny Ed, we figure you've helped us in a tough situation. If you really mean it, we would be glad to have you coach the Raiders tomorrow night."

Granny Ed's face broke into a smile bright enough to light up all the western states. "Gentlemen," she said, in a choked voice, "you're going to be the winner."

Darby was three times the size of Lewisville, and their big gym was packed to the rafters as we made our entrance. Last one in the door was Granny Ed, her knitting bag under one arm and chalkboard under the other. She sat down primly on the Lewisville bench, placed her knitting bag beside her, the chalkboard on the floor, and, folding her hands in her lap, watched intently every move we were making in warm-ups.

"I'm sorry, madam," the Darby coach said, moving toward Granny Ed. "This bench is reserved for the Lewisville Raiders and their coach. You'll have to move up in the stands with the other spectators."

"Young man, I am perfectly fine right here," Granny Ed said, gently pushing the Darby coach aside to watch our warm-ups.

"Don't you understand what I'm saying? Only the coach can sit here," he repeated loudly.

"Don't shout, young man. I heard you the first time. For your information, I *am* the coach," Granny Ed said, standing as tall as her five feet would stretch.

"You're what?" the Darby coach gasped. "You said you're what?" he repeated as though his hearing had failed.

"You heard me correctly. Now, if you will kindly move out of my way, I should like very much to watch my team's warm-up."

"This is absolutely unbelievable! I can't put my players out on the floor to play a little old lady's team."

"Well, I shall assume that if your team doesn't show up on the floor when the game whistle blows, you will forfeit the game to the Lewisville Raiders," Granny offered sweetly.

"Forfeit!" the Darby coach shouted. "We'll forfeit nothing. Just remember, Coach Whatever-yournameis, you'll be treated the same as any other coach, even if you *are* a woman." He stamped back and plopped himself down on the far end of the Darby bench.

"Hothead, isn't he?" Granny Ed said with a twinkle in her eye. I knew right then Granny Ed had psyched out our first opponent.

Our fast break was super that night, and using a two-platoon system, Granny Ed directed a complete rout of the Darby Bulldogs. When the game ended, the scoreboard read: Lewisville–85; Darby–55. It was the upset of the year, and one the people in Lewisville are still talking about.

At the end of the game, Granny Ed gathered up her knitting bag and her chalkboard. She walked quickly to the Darby coach for the traditional handshake and commented ever so sweetly, "The name is not Whateveryournameis, young man. The name is Granny Ed, coach of the Lewisville Raiders."

The Darby coach flinched, turned, and fled to the Darby dressing room. It was the Darby win that launched Granny Ed in her coaching career.

Our Lewisville Raiders, with Granny Ed as head coach, breezed through the fourteen-game league schedule undefeated; and we qualified for the state tournament. Granny Ed had become a celebrity throughout the state. Our phone rang with interview requests and well-wishers. Granny Ed seemed to thrive on all the excitement and was happier than I'd ever seen her.

The state tournament was serious business to Granny Ed, and our practices were no-nonsense and hard work. Next week, our team would travel to the city for our town's first appearance in a state tournament. Then we would find out if the Lewisville Raiders were really good or only a much-publicized curiosity.

The night before we left for the tournament, Granny Ed came into my room and sank down on the bed. Her usual smiling face was drawn and lined. "Sprout, I'm afraid this time I've overstepped my bounds. It was all right to coach against schools in our league, but next week we'll be competing against the big boys. I'm not sure I'm up to it. Maybe it's time for me to step aside."

I folded and refolded the shirt I was packing before I dared look up at her. "Granny Ed, you've taken us this far. Don't you think you owe it to the team to stay with us when the going gets rough?"

"It isn't that I don't want to. I just hope I don't let the team down." Managing a weak smile, she stood up and headed for the door. "Well, with the team behind me, and you behind me, and my picture splashed over half the newspapers in the state, there's just no telling what will happen. Right, Sprout?"

I gave her a big wink. "Granny Ed, nobody ever would have guessed we'd get this far. We'll give it all we've got and every one we win is for you."

"King City, here we come!" Leftie shouted as the

chartered bus, decorated from front to back with gaudy red and gold banners, entered the city limits. There was no turning back now. For better or for worse, our team was about to play in its first state tourney. *Heaven help us and Granny Ed!* I thought. *And Grandpa Thor, if you have any pull up there, don't let the other teams pour it on too bad.*

Each team in the tournament was given a practice session in the Coliseum before it competed in its first game. The Coliseum was unbelievably big. It seated 10,000, which was about 9,500 more than the Lewisville gym. Granny Ed could tell how nervous we all were.

"Gentlemen," she said, motioning for us to join her at the side of the gym floor. "You will notice that the playing floor is exactly the same size as our floor. The basket is precisely the same height from the floor. And according to my calculations, it should take no more energy to run up and down this floor, and put the ball through the hoop, than it does in our gym. Am I right?"

A resounding "Right!" was her answer.

With a twinkle in her eyes, Granny Ed went on, "Then I can assume, gentlemen, the player who is not able to do this effectively isn't putting out his all, and I shall personally jab that player with my knitting needle where it will do the most good. Right?"

That broke the team up and they shouted an even louder "Right!"

She had psyched the team out of a bad case of jitters. The only thing was . . . how long would it be before our magic bubble burst?

No one was more surprised or happy than Granny Ed and the Raider team when we swept with ease through the first three games on the winning side. By now, the Lewisville Raiders had become the Cinderella team of the tournament, the country bumpkins showing the city boys the finer points of the game. Headlines in the papers praised our team and Granny Ed.

GRANNY ED AND HER RIPPIN' RAIDERS WIN AGAIN met our eyes as we passed the newspaper stand. We headed for the last and final game—our chance for the state championship.

I don't know who kept the town going, or if they closed up completely, because I saw most of the people of Lewisville packed in the stands. The town's oldest resident, Emil Gunder, was waving a sign saying: GIVE IT TO 'EM, GRANNY.

"Look at that old fool," Granny Ed nudged and whispered to me as she spied Old Emil waving his sign; yet I noticed a smile of satisfaction on her face from the show of support.

The buzzer sounded to start the game. Granny Ed slowly looked around the circle of ballplayers.

"Well, gentlemen, this is it! This is the big one we've been waiting to play. It's the whole ball of wax this time." She gave us a big wink and added, "Don't forget, I've got my secret weapon." And she pointed to the knitting needle neatly tucked in her braids.

I won't say the Orolatch team was tall. Let's put it this way. I'm six-feet, three-inches tall, and it strained my neck to look up at the forward I was to guard. The center opposite Al looked like Paul Bunyan's cousin, and I had the feeling that if he landed on Al, we would find only a splat on the floor where Al had once been. Such were the odds when the Lewisville Raiders played the Orolatch Tigers.

The team managed to stay even with Orolatch due to our fantastic shooting percentage during the first half. Leftie proved to be a deadeye, and we trailed by only two points at the end of the third quarter. The noise was terrific, and the tension was thick enough to cut. The fact that fouls were not being called closely added to the chaos. Al looked as though he'd been through a meat grinder. The big Orolatch center had worked him over with his elbows and knees.

I glanced at the bench and noticed Granny Ed was getting kind of purple-red in the face. The last straw was when the Orolatch center, driving to the basket, knocked Al flat, and the referee called the foul on Al who was lying on the floor.

"Basket counts!" the referee yelled, "and a foul on number twenty-three." A flash of red tennis shoes streaked toward the surprised referee. The rest I wish I could forget.

"Sir, and I use that term loosely," Granny Ed shouted, glaring angrily up at the face of the referee, "I brought a team on the floor to play basketball, not to have them dismembered. That asinine call only strengthens my belief that you are *blind!*" And with that she stripped her wire-framed glasses from her face and handed them to the dumbfounded referee.

There was a dead silence as he stared in disbelief at the small, gray-haired figure marching back to the Lewisville bench. Then it happened!

"Technical foul on the Raider bench!" he shouted, making the dreaded *T* sign with his hands and pointing straight at Granny Ed.

The big center missed his foul shots, but the Orolatch guard calmly stepped to the line and sank the technical. I looked up at the scoreboard. Two minutes in the game and Orolatch led 75–70. Well, we came close, I thought.

The Orolatch coach called timeout. It was pretty

obvious what his strategy would be with only two minutes left.

"They will no doubt go into a stall," Granny Ed said. "Our only chance is to press and press hard. We've got to get possession of that ball!"

Leftie stole the out-of-bounds play and streaked the full length of the court for a lay-in. The crowd erupted with a deafening roar.

This time the Orolatch team passed the ball inbounds and were able to stall for a minute and a half before Al fouled the big center in a frantic try for the ball.

The big center swaggered to the foul line. His shot rolled round and round the rim and *off*. I timed my jump for the rebound perfectly, and that's the last thing I remember. The big guy had crashed into me. How I held the ball is a miracle, for I was sure my head must be lying somewhere underneath the basket.

"You hurt Sprout?" Granny Ed's voice was anxious as she bent over me on the floor. I shook my head feebly, although I wasn't sure all my body parts were still connected.

"All right then," she whispered in my ear, "you've got a one and one foul shot coming up, and we have no timeouts left. Make the first one and miss the second one. Al will rebound and score a field goal. There are only nine seconds left. Do you understand?"

I nodded weakly. Understand! Understand! Just like that I was to make the first free throw. There was a small matter of my being only a .500 freethrow shooter. Had Granny Ed taken that into consideration? I motioned to Al as I dragged my bruised body to the opposite end of the gym. I whispered Granny

Ed's wild game plan to him. He nodded matter-of-factly and stationed himself along the side of the basket.

Shaking my head to clear out the spinning wheels, I stepped to the foul line. "This is crazy," I thought. I see two baskets up there. Now which one shall I aim for? I chose the top one in my half-conscious state and carefully arched the ball upward.

Swish! Down through the net it sailed. The noise of the crowd seemed very far away. *Now miss this one.* Granny Ed's words cut through the fog in my brain. I aimed the ball for the rim of the basket, and then I did something I've never told anyone—not even Granny Ed. I closed my eyes—tight. I never saw what happened in those last hectic seconds, but I heard a shriek erupt from the Lewisville fans.

"Fouled in the act of shooting!" the referee croaked. Al had rebounded and scored the field goal. He was gently pushing me aside to shoot the one shot that could win the ball game. Pandemonium broke loose. We'd won! The unbelievable had happened! Lewisville had won the State Championship! The team lifted Granny Ed to their shoulders and marched triumphantly out on the floor. She waved happily to the Lewisville rooters. As the players set her down, she grabbed my arm and whispered, "Big Thor should have been here! He always loved the tough ones."

Then a weird thing happened. The lights in that huge Coliseum dimmed, flickered, and came back on.

Granny Ed winked at me and said confidently, "He knows." And do you know something? I'm not so sure he doesn't.

A Game of Catch

by Richard Wilbur

As Lincoln and Monica found out, a simple game of basketball can have unforeseen consequences. The characters in this short story play a game of catch. How do you account for the unusual twist this story takes?

Monk and Glennie were playing catch on the side lawn of the firehouse when Scho caught sight of them. They were good at it, for seventh-graders, as anyone could see right away. Monk, wearing a catcher's mitt, would lean easily sidewise and back, with one leg lifted and his throwing hand almost down to the grass, and then lob the white ball straight up into the sunlight. Glennie would shield his eyes with his left hand and, just as the ball fell past him, snag it with a little dart of his glove. Then he would burn the ball straight toward Monk, and it would spank into the round mitt and sit, like a still-life apple on a plate, until Monk flipped it over into his right hand and, with a negligent flick of his hanging arm, gave Glennie a fast grounder.

They were going on and on like that, in a kind of slow, mannered, luxurious dance in the sun, their faces perfectly blank and entranced, when Glennie noticed Scho dawdling along the other side of the street and called hello to him. Scho crossed over and stood at the front edge of the lawn, near an apple tree, watching.

"Got your glove?" asked Glennie after a time. Scho obviously hadn't.

"You could give me some easy grounders," said Scho. "But don't burn 'em."

"All right," Glennie said. He moved off a little, so the three of them formed a triangle, and they passed the ball around for about five minutes, Monk tossing easy grounders to Scho, Scho throwing to Glennie, and Glennie burning them in to Monk. After a while, Monk began to throw them back to Glennie once or twice before he let Scho have his grounder, and finally Monk gave Scho a fast, bumpy grounder that hopped over his shoulder and went into the brake on the other side of the street.

"Not so hard," called Scho as he ran across to get it.

"You should've had it," Monk shouted.

It took Scho a little while to find the ball among the ferns and dead leaves, and when he saw it, he grabbed it up and threw it toward Glennie. It struck the trunk of the apple tree, bounced back at an angle, and rolled steadily and stupidly onto the cement apron in front of the firehouse, where one of the trucks was parked. Scho ran hard and stopped it just before it rolled under the truck, and this time he carried it back to his former position on the lawn and threw it carefully to Glennie.

"I got an idea," said Glennie. "Why don't Monk and I catch for five minutes more, and then you can borrow one of our gloves?"

"That's all right with me," said Monk. He socked his fist into his mitt, and Glennie burned one in.

"All right," Scho said, and went over and sat under the tree. There in the shade he watched them resume their skillful play. They threw lazily fast or lazily slow—high, low, or wide—and always handsomely, their expressions serene, changeless, and forgetful. When Monk missed a low backhand catch, he walked indolently after the ball and, hardly even looking, flung it sidearm for an imaginary put-out. After a good while of this, Scho said, "Isn't it five minutes yet?"

"One minute to go," said Monk, with a fraction of a grin.

Scho stood up and watched the ball slap back and forth for several minutes more, and then he turned and pulled himself up into the crotch of the tree.

"Where you going?" Monk asked.

"Just up the tree," Scho said.

"I guess he doesn't want to catch," said Monk.

Scho went up and up through the fat light-gray branches until they grew slender and bright and gave under him. He found a place where several supple branches were knit to make a dangerous chair, and sat there with his head coming out of the leaves into the sunlight. He could see the two other boys down below, the ball going back and forth between them as if they were bowling on the grass, and Glennie's crew-cut head looking like a sea urchin.

"I found a wonderful seat up here," Scho said loudly. "If I don't fall out." Monk and Glennie didn't look up or comment, and so he began jouncing gently in his chair of branches and singing "Yo-ho, heave ho" in an exaggerated way.

"Do you know what, Monk?" he announced in a few moments. "I can make you two guys do anything I want. Catch that ball, Monk! Now you catch it, Glennie!"

"I was going to catch it anyway," Monk suddenly said. "You're not making anybody do anything when they're already going to do it anyway."

"I made you say what you just said," Scho replied joyfully.

"No, you didn't," said Monk, still throwing and catching but now less serenely absorbed in the game.

"That's what I wanted you to say," Scho said.

The ball bounded off the rim of Monk's mitt and plowed into a gladiolus bed beside the firehouse, and Monk ran to get it while Scho jounced in his treetop and sang, "I wanted you to miss that. Anything you do is what I wanted you to do."

"Let's quit for a minute," Glennie suggested.

"We might as well, until the peanut gallery shuts up," Monk said.

They went over and sat cross-legged in the shade of the tree. Scho looked down between his legs and saw them on the dim, spotty ground, saying nothing to one another. Glennie soon began abstractedly spinning his glove between his palms; Monk pulled his nose and stared out across the lawn.

"I want you to mess around with your nose, Monk," said Scho, giggling. Monk withdrew his hand from his face.

"Do that with your glove, Glennie," Scho persisted. "Monk, I want you to pull up hunks of grass and chew on it."

Glennie looked up and saw a self-delighted, intense face staring down at him through the leaves. "Stop being a dope and come down and we'll catch for a few minutes," he said.

Scho hesitated, and then said, in a tentatively mocking voice, "That's what I wanted you to say."

"All right, then, nuts to you," said Glennie.

"Why don't you keep quiet and stop bothering people?" Monk asked.

"I made you say that," Scho replied, softly.

"Shut up," Monk said.

"I made you say that, and I want you to be standing there looking sore. And I want you to climb up the tree. I'm making you do it!"

Monk was scrambling up through the branches, awkward in his haste, and getting snagged on twigs. His face was furious and foolish, and he kept telling Scho to shut up, shut up, shut up, while the other's exuberant and panicky voice poured down upon his head.

"*Now* you shut up or you'll be sorry," Monk said, breathing hard as he reached up and threatened to shake the cradle of slight branches in which Scho was sitting.

"I *want*—" Scho screamed as he fell. Two lower branches broke his rustling, crackling fall, but he landed on his back with a deep thud and lay still, with a strangled look on his face and his eyes clenched. Glennie knelt down and asked breathlessly, "Are you O.K., Scho? Are you O.K.?," while Monk swung down through the leaves crying that honestly he hadn't even touched him, the crazy guy just let go. Scho doubled up and turned over on his right side, and now both the other boys knelt beside him, pawing at his shoulder and begging to know how he was.

Then Scho rolled away from them and sat partly up, still struggling to get his wind but forcing a species of smile onto his face.

"I'm sorry, Scho," Monk said. "I didn't mean to make you fall."

Scho's voice came out weak and gravelly, in gasps. "I meant—you to do it. You—had to. You can't do—anything—unless I want—you to."

Glennie and Monk looked helplessly at him as he sat there, breathing a bit more easily and smiling fixedly, with tears in his eyes. Then they picked up their gloves and the ball, walked over to the street, and went slowly away down the sidewalk, Monk punching his fist into the mitt, Glennie juggling the ball between glove and hand.

From under the apple tree, Scho, still bent over a little for lack of breath, croaked after them in triumph and misery, "I want you to do whatever you're going to do for the whole rest of your life!"